COMMON SENSE ABOUT AFRICA

COMMON SENSE ABOUT
AFRICA

by
ANTHONY SAMPSON

NEW YORK
THE MACMILLAN COMPANY
1960

CONTENTS

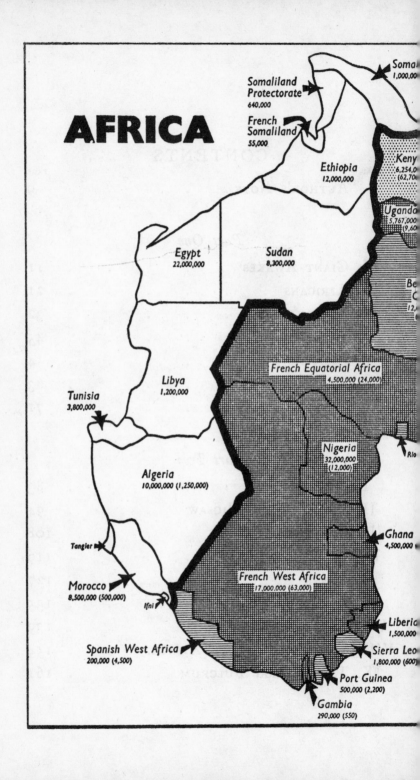

AFRICA

Somal 1,000,00

Somaliland Protectorate 640,000

French Somaliland 55,000

Ethiopia 12,000,000

Keny 6,254,0 (62,70

Ugand 5,767,000 (9,60

Egypt 22,000,000

Sudan 8,300,000

Be C 12,

French Equatorial Africa 4,500,000 (24,000)

Libya 1,200,000

Tunisia 3,800,000

Nigeria 32,000,000 (12,000)

Rio

Algeria 10,000,000 (1,250,000)

Tangier

Ghana 4,500,000

Morocco 8,500,000 (500,000)

Ifni

French West Africa 17,000,000 (63,000)

Liberia 1,500,000

Sierra Leo 1,800,000 (600

Spanish West Africa 200,000 (4,500)

Port Guinea 500,000 (2,200)

Gambia 290,000 (550)

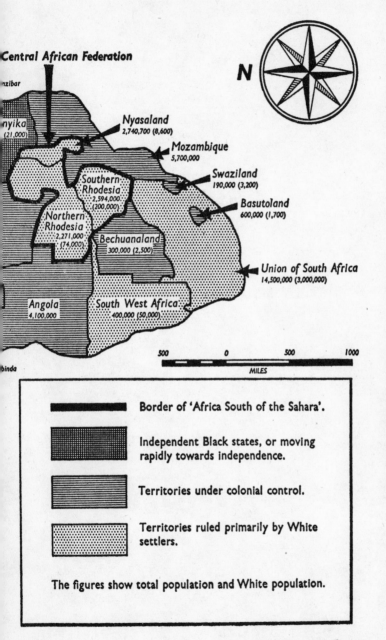

Central African Federation

nzibar

nyika
(21,000)

Nyasaland
2,740,700 (8,600)

Mozambique
5,700,000

Swaziland
190,000 (3,200)

Southern
Rhodesia
2,594,000
(200,000)

Basutoland
600,000 (1,700)

Northern
Rhodesia
2,271,000
(74,000)

Bechuanaland
300,000 (2,500)

Union of South Africa
14,500,000 (3,000,000)

Angola
4,100,000

South West Africa
400,000 (50,000)

N

500   0   500   1000

MILES

binda

Border of 'Africa South of the Sahara'.

Independent Black states, or moving
rapidly towards independence.

Territories under colonial control.

Territories ruled primarily by White
settlers.

The figures show total population and White population.

Jeffery Matthews

AUTHOR'S NOTE

THIS BOOK IS ABOUT 'Africa South of the Sahara',
or 'Black Africa', as it is sometimes called. The division is in many ways an artificial one, and it excludes
such countries as Somalia and the Sudan, which are
having an increasing influence on their neighbours:
but the field of 'Arab Africa' across the North of the
continent is a separate study, and connected more
closely with the Middle East than with the rest of
the continent.

Even with this exclusion, the problems of trying to
compress the continent into 45,000 words are quite
formidable. There is no central government or policy
as in Russia or China, and the different countries are
at least as diverse as those of Europe. Faced with this
complexity, I have not attempted to give each country
its fair share of text. I make no apology for giving
Nigeria less attention than Ghana, which has an eighth
of its population but which at present has more apparent fame and symbolic importance. Inevitably, the
countries where there is most trouble and danger have
attracted the most attention, and the racial conflicts of
the East and South tend in the newspapers to eclipse
the progress of the West.

In so far that Africa has a connecting theme, it is
African nationalism, which must form the main *motif*
of this book. The preponderance of politics leaves little
room for Animal Africa, Explorers' Africa, Engineers'
Africa or even Missionary Africa. I have tried—as far
as possible in this quickly-changing field—to give a

general picture of the continent to-day, without dwelling too long on its past: the book is therefore much more concerned with Black Africa than with White.

In the first half I have dealt with the general characteristics of the continent as a whole: in the second part I have rapidly surveyed the problems of the separate territories, from West to East to South, concluding with the nub of Central Africa. I am acutely aware that, in trying to give a bold picture of the continent, I have had to make drastic oversimplifications and omissions.

In a book with such wide focus, my debts to other books, to reports, correspondents and conversations, are too many to be properly acknowledged. But for corrections and advice, I owe particular thanks to Shirley Williams, Mary Benson, Clyde Sanger, Hella Pick, Michael Faber and Robin Denniston.

LONDON,
October 1959.

PART ONE

CHAPTER I

GIANT AWAKES

No one now doubts that the whole of Africa is waking up. It is changing so fast, not simply in events but in its whole character, that history books become out of date in a year. Since 1945, when the continent seemed stable and settled, with little thought of African independence, nearly every territory has suffered a major upset. The names that now make news in the continent—Mboya, Nkrumah, Verwoerd, Welensky, Sekou Touré—were in 1945 merely members of unknown oppositions.

But the greatest changes are still to come, and many of them will be associated with the new millennium in African history—1960. It will be an *annus mirabilis* without precedent in the continent. The biggest nation in Africa, Nigeria, will become independent, and so half Britain's colonial population will disappear overnight. The French Cameroons, underneath Nigeria, and French Togoland, next door to Ghana, will both end their period of trusteeship.

At the other end of the continent, the Federation of Central Africa (the Rhodesias and Nyasaland) will have its constitution reviewed in London. Kenya, too, will have a constitutional conference. And in these uneasy surroundings, South Africa will celebrate in 1960 the jubilee of its Union.

The three territories of British East Africa will be
moving towards independence, led probably by Tanganyika. The block of French territories underneath
the Sahara will have become self-governing within the
French community, and may well follow, one by one,
the independence of French Guinea. Even the Belgian
Congo, which for years has been assumed to be insulated against the clamour for self-government, has under-
gone a rapid change of direction. Only the Portuguese
territories, Angola in the West and Mozambique in the
East, have so far resisted the pressures towards change.

The new map of Africa will therefore be scarcely
recognizable, and the old one largely irrelevant. In the
South, there will be a bastion of white supremacy, at
loggerheads with the continent further north. In the
West, there will be strongholds of black power, which
the neighbouring states will find difficult to ignore. In
the East, there will be diversified African states, complicated by white and Indian minorities, and by tribal
frictions, but committed to eventual independence.
Between them will be unquiet multi-racial countries,
such as the Congo, pulled towards both poles.

Africa's independence makes it a quite different
study. In the days of settled colonial rule, the capitals
of Africa were London, Paris or Brussels; in the continent itself there was hardly any international diplomacy, and important decisions came always from
the metropoles. African governments were thus dull:
the whole of British Africa had a facial resemblance,
usually with a Governor, a Legislative Council, and
an Executive Council, carrying out the policy of the
Colonial Office in London. In all the territories, wild
or eccentric though they might be, there were the

same clubs, the same imported colonial architecture, the same gymkhanas and garden-parties, throwing a uniform white sheet over the black life underneath. Now that the sheet is being pulled away, the continent is uncovered. Watching Africa deciding its fate has the same kind of fascination as watching schoolboys after they have been liberated from school.

Africa is coming out of the tunnel—not necessarily into bright light, but certainly to a more varied scenery. The tunnel has not been a long one, but the shape of the world has been transformed in the interim. It is only sixty-five years since Uganda was declared a protectorate in 1894, and it seems likely that it will return to independence within one man's lifetime: but the Uganda of the nineteen-sixties will hardly be recognizable—except in some important relics—as the isolated and skin-clad people which Lugard moulded together in the 1890's. Ashantiland was only annexed by Britain in 1901, to become part of independent Ghana fifty-six years later. Between 1885, when the European Powers first 'scrambled' for Africa at the Congress of Berlin, and 1957, when Ghana achieved her independence, was the brief period when black Africa was wholly under white domination.

It is only since the last war that Africa has been considered by the West as an important continent worthy of inclusion with the other five. Its neglect in pre-war histories and journalism seems now astonishing: it was regarded as a kind of poor man's India, a backyard of the Empire. What reports there were, were largely concerned with the conflicts between Whites, and the extension of European politics into Africa. But since the Second World War, everything has happened at once to make Africa important : much of Asia has disappeared behind the Iron Curtain, nationalism has burnt through the world, and Africa has become more wealthy and valuable. The small-nation diplomacy of the United Nations and the formation of the 'Afro-Asian Bloc' of uncommitted countries between Russia and America has brought Africa into a sudden new role for the West. From being regarded as an awkward chattel, hanging down from Europe, Africa now finds herself being wooed and counter-wooed as the 'last great diplomatic prize', the 'last frontier' and the 'Uncommitted Continent'.

The boom of interest in Africa, which has so astonished publishers and travel-agents, is based on excellent reasons. From being a kind of huge zoo, or 'musée vivant', as the French call it, it has changed into a busy political laboratory, experimenting with all the theories and ideals of the rest of the world. The absorption of Western ideas into Africa, combined with the strangeness of the surroundings, gives it a special fascination for the people of the West, as an unfamiliar mirror-image.

While the rest of the world was discovering Africa's importance, Africans were discovering it for themselves. It happened with amazing speed : nearly all the serious African movements have sprung up since the war. It now seems more surprising that Africans had not woken up earlier; but if Colonial Governors were taken aback by the quickness of the changes, they cannot altogether be blamed. Ghana, Nigeria, Kenya, Uganda, Tanganyika, Nyasaland and Northern Rhodesia, all formed their first nationalist organizations within a few post-war years.

Since then, African enthusiasm and confidence has grown by leaps and bounds—reinforced by the discovery that, at the first sign of serious pressure, colonial powers were likely to give way. 'Hands Off Africa', 'The Giant Awakes!', 'Africa shall be free'—the slogans have rung round the continent, echoing from one territory to the next. From the first improbable demands of Kwame Nkrumah in the Gold Coast in 1948, the idea of African freedom has become in ten years an accepted fact. From the ideal of national independence has now developed the ideal of Panafrica—of a great United States of Africa (or 'Commonwealth of Africa', as it is variously referred to) which will unite the continent into another America—a continent that will be the paragon of the world. Behind this Panafrican pride there is the belief that, as the last continent to achieve its freedom, Africa can benefit from the rest of the world's mistakes, and can inherit, unencumbered by previous centuries, all the riches and opportunities of the twentieth. As Africa had enriched the rest of the world in the past, so now the rest of the world might enrich Africa, to create a great new continent.

What was the alarm-bell which broke the African sleep? There were several causes, and it is difficult to put them in order of importance. First, probably, was the war itself, which spread ideas of human rights, allowed more than a quarter of a million British and French Africans to travel, and loosened the West's hold on Africa: the independence of India was a challenge to Africans to achieve the same. Second, was the maturing of a new generation of educated Africans, educated mainly in Britain and America—Nkrumah, Kenyatta, Azikiwe, Banda, Nyerere, Nkumbula—who had modern, confident ideas of organization and agitation. Third, perhaps, was the growth of the African working class in the towns, with newspapers, wirelesses and cinemas to teach them about their nations and potentialities. Fourth, was the loss of confidence by the colonial powers themselves, who had neither the will nor the troops to maintain a reluctant and dangerous African empire. That the lack of will was more important than the lack of troops is suggested by the fact that the two powers which have held their African possessions most firmly—Belgium and Portugal—have been two of the weakest.

Of Africa's importance there can be no doubt: it has grown, and will grow, beyond recognition. Many of its natural disadvantages—its lack of rivers, harbours and fertile regions, its tsetse-fly areas, its dearth of communications, which have all accounted for its past backwardness—can be overcome by modern methods. But in the prevailing enthusiasm about Africa, it is important to keep it in perspective.

It is true that it is enormous—11,262,000 square miles, bigger than Russia or all North America: but its wealth and importance bear very little relationship to its size. It is a giant, but a flabby giant, with only a few muscles and sinews. It was not till the last century that Europeans became interested in the mere acreage of Africa—before that it was regarded as an awkward obstacle on the way to India, with a few stretches of useful coastline: 'a coast, not a continent'. It was Rhodes, as much as anyone, who became interested in chunks of Africa for their own sake, and determined to carve a route from Cape to Cairo. "Every man has his foible", said Lord Milner:

"Rhodes' foible was size." But the achievements of 'red on the map' became a very widespread foible: and it could never be predicted when some apparently useless outpost, like the copper corner of Northern Rhodesia, might not prove a huge source of wealth.

The population is lumped in a few isolated heaps. The latest census estimates about two hundred million people in the whole of Africa (including five million Europeans): but a demographic map shows most of them accumulated in three main clusters: in Nigeria; in East Africa, between Lake Victoria and Lake Tanganyika; and round the gold reef of Johannesburg. There is a thin layer of population along the South-east coast, and on the underside of the West Coast. Outside these concentrated groups, most of Africa is incredibly empty: it is possible to fly over it for two hours without seeing a house, and with no change of scenery.

Most of the wealth of Africa comes from a series of economic 'islands' as they are called, where production is concentrated: it has been estimated that 4 per cent of the area of Tropical Africa produces 85 per cent of its exports.[1] The gold and uranium reefs of Johannesburg and the Orange Free State, the copper-belt of Northern Rhodesia and the Congo, and the secondary industries of South Africa and Southern Rhodesia have absorbed nearly half the foreign capital arriving in Africa since the war.

In spite of its advances, Africa is still desperately poor: the whole continent exports only 4 per cent of the world's raw materials. Because more than half of

[1] William A. Hance: African Economic Development. Oxford, 1958.

the population is still under a subsistence economy in which no money changes hands, it is impossible to compare accurately its income with other continents : but the Gross National Product of Africa has been estimated at about four billion pounds, or rather less than a quarter that of Britain, for four times its population. In British East Africa, the average income per family is ten pounds a year; in the whole continent less than 10 per cent of the people can read or write.

The idea current among Africans, that European supremacy and the industrial revolution were built on the riches of Africa and slave labour, does not stand up to history. British Victorian standards of living were certainly helped by the addition of African trade : but the capital which built the Industrial Revolution came from cheap labour inside Britain, and owed little to the slave trade. Africa was not then rich enough to be really valuable to Europe, and it was not till the discovery of gold and diamonds that it attracted high finance.

Nor does the political development of Africa, unfortunately, have a necessary connection with economic advance : the most rapidly developing areas are still the countries—South Africa, Rhodesia, the Congo— under white domination. A survey by *The Economist*,[1] estimating that the modernization of a backward territory needed 15 per cent of the national income to be devoted to productive investment, found that only in the Congo, Rhodesias and South Africa—all three of them white dominated—had this figure been reached.

Closely connected with economic progress are the

[1] 'The African Revolution', *The Economist*, December 13, 1958.

railways : "the material development of Africa", said
Lord Lugard, "may be summed up in one word—
transport". Railways in Africa, however, are so appal-
lingly expensive that only the prospect of great wealth
at the other end drives them on. Diamonds brought
the railway to Kimberley, gold brought it to Johannesburg, and copper to Northern Rhodesia. But once a
railway is built, it is the life-line of all kinds of agricultural and industrial development. One of the few
railways which was built with no obvious purpose, the
line to Uganda (of which it was said at the time :

> What is the use of it none can conjecture
> What it will carry there's none can define . . .)

has been the foundation of Kenya's prosperity. But
white men and railways are inclined to go together ;
settlers were first introduced to Kenya largely to provide trade for the railways, and white settlements in
Rhodesia are dotted along the 'line of rail' to the
copper-belt. By far the most impressive network of
railways and transport in the continent is in the Union
of South Africa. With railways can come all the amenities of housing, training and rapid movement which
go under the general heading of 'infrastructure'—the
framework of transport and organization without which
there can be no quick economic advance, however
much money is poured in.

In spite of their support for African independence,
British and American investors still prefer, partly for
these reasons, partly from their fear of expropriation
or chaos in nationalistic states, to put their money into
territories under white control. Though South Africa
has recently become too restrictive to encourage new

capital, the two regions developing most rapidly in Africa are the two white-controlled areas of Rhodesia and the Congo. Compared to these, investment in Ghana or Uganda is tiny.

The fact that black political progress is not necessarily followed by economic progress is very awkward. It is still broadly true that 'whosoever hath, to him shall be given': and the younger African states are so dependent on single commodities exported to the West —cocoa in Ghana, sisal in Tanganyika, cotton in Uganda—that with a setback in trade they could quickly become poorer. There is no sign of a 'great leap forward', on the scale of Russia or China, in Black Africa.

Investment from the West is still the main source of African prosperity and rising standards of living; and however much the idea of an undeveloped Africa —the 'Happy Haiti' attitude, as it has been called[1]— may appeal to European tourists, it has little attraction for Africans. The prospect of black poverty side by side with white riches, in a continent beset with pride and resentments, is full of international dangers; and the problem facing the West, of how to develop the new Black Africa as effectively as it has developed the old White Africa, is now the most pressing of all.

[1] Arthur Gaitskell: *What Have They to Defend?*, Africa Bureau, 1955.

CHAPTER II

AFRICANS

THE MAIN COMMON FACTOR in Black Africa is, of course, that it contains Africans. But Africans, about whom so many generalizations have been made, are at least as varied as Europeans : and until recently, an African from the East Coast, for instance, hardly ever came into contact with a West African : while Africans in South Africa are still almost entirely cut off from the continent further north. It is only their common contrast with Whites that has made them look alike : and now that white domination is ending, the differences and conflicts between Africans are rapidly becoming apparent.

Even the word 'African' is itself very vague, and in the East and South it is a comparatively new coinage to replace the old words 'Native', 'Kaffir', 'Munt' or 'Nigger', which are still commonly used by local Whites, but are considered insulting by Africans. The nomenclature for the inhabitants of the continent is still an embarrassment, since the word 'African' is obviously ambiguous—particularly in its Dutch translation, *Afrikaner*. 'South African' is commonly taken in England to mean a white South African, and therefore awkward phrases like 'African South African' or 'South African African' are needed to describe the other three-quarters of the inhabitants.

The confusion over the meaning of 'African' is part of the confusion over the last few decades as to whom the country really belongs to: and there is almost equal confusion over the use of the word 'European', which is used in South Africa to describe people who have lived out of Europe for three centuries. Fortunately, with the rise of African pride and nationalism, the straightforward adjective 'black' is becoming more acceptable to Africans, though as a noun it is still often regarded as derogatory. French-educated Africans, who have a more confident sense of equality, are less touchy about the use of the word *noir*; and it seems likely that, as racial feelings become easier, the people of the continent will be described more and more as 'Blacks' and 'Whites', which is how they first appear to each other.

But not all Africans by any means are black. They are normally divided into two main categories—Negroes and Bantu. The Negroes, who number around forty-five million, come from West Africa above the line of the 'bulge', and are comparatively very dark: it was from there that the American and West Indian slaves were taken. The Bantu are thought to be a mixture of the Negroes and the Hamites, the light-skinned people who probably came from Arabia and now survive mainly round the Horn of Africa. Bantu itself is a very rough classification, referring to language, not race: all Bantu use the suffix *-ntu* to mean *man*. In South Africa 'Bantu' is used as a polite word, particularly by Afrikaners, to mean 'Africans'; but Africans are inclined to object to it, partly because it is used by Afrikaners, partly because—as they say—it sounds like part of the flora and fauna.

Bantu, being mixed, are usually lighter than Negroes, sometimes very light, often with quite European features. It is broadly true that the further south, the lighter the Africans: to see a Xhosa from the Cape in South Africa next to an Ashanti from Northern Ghana is to realize how inaccurate the word 'black' is to describe the Bantu. Black South Africans, who are very colour-conscious as a result of the colour bar, often jokingly refer to the Nyasas who come down to work from the north as 'niggers'.

Apart from this racial confusion, Africans have developed variously according to their different surroundings and histories. The division between the East and West is the sharpest of all: there is no railway line across the continent, and the road through the Congo is passable for only half the year.

Within the territories the differences between Africans are almost as acute. It is not only that there are many hundreds of different tribes—speaking about seven hundred different languages—often with a past tradition of fighting, exploiting or dominating each other. There is also the fundamental contrast between urban and rural people, between peasants and factory workers, or between university graduates and illiterates. The impressions that a journalist, for instance, gains of a country by talking to a tiny minority of African lawyers and politicians, and the impression of a settler-housewife who talks only to her servants, are equally misleading.

One situation is common to nearly all Africans— the conflict between the old African and the new, between the pristine tribal way of life and the new de-tribalized existence of the cities, industry and trade. Almost the whole of Black Africa has been ruled by hereditary chiefs, of varying powers—ranging from grand autocratic kingdoms, such as the Kabaka's in Uganda or the Ashantehene's in Ghana, to small chieftancies binding together a few villages. The whole life of the old Africa revolved round the Chief—his witch-doctors, ancestors, fetishes and ceremonials.

In parts, his power was modified by councils of elders or gatherings of the tribe, who were able to criticize and influence his actions with some semblance of democracy; the strong sense of community, particularly communal ownership of land, is often held to be a reason for the lack of success of communist doctrines in Africa. Several educated Chiefs, notably in East Africa, have succeeded in making the awkward transition from autocratic rulers to progressive, democratic heads. But the influence of the Chiefs has on the whole been at least as conservative as the House of Lords, and opposed to the spread of democracy and votes.

The colonial powers have found it convenient in the past to use the hierarchy of chiefs as an instrument of rule, and even to strengthen them: the principle of 'indirect rule' as it is called, was first organized, out of sheer necessity, by Lord Lugard in Northern Nigeria after 1900, where there was a strong Moslem ruling class and a tiny band of British administrators. But rule through Chiefs was soon extended to most other British territories, including Kikuyuland in Kenya, where Chiefs had to be invented. The Belgians split up the number of Chiefs in the Congo to over two thousand, and now use them as tax-collectors and civil servants, with government salaries. The South African Government use chiefs as their paid agents, who can be (and are) dismissed if they are disobedient.

This association of the Chiefs with foreign powers

has made them increasingly unpopular with the new leaders of the masses, and has sharpened the conflict between the two sides of African life. The British fondness for chiefs was originally largely a matter of expediency: they saved the administration a great deal of manpower and trouble. But there were also human reasons: Europeans have always preferred the ancient tribal Africa to the new cities, which are more troublesome, and too like industrial cities anywhere else in the world. The friendship between the old-style District Commissioner and 'his chief' was a real one: the white man often respected the dignity and grandeur of the tribal ruler, and loved the unchanging order which he represented. The fact that the more senior chiefs were often educated in England, or in the African equivalent of English public schools, made the bond still firmer. Northern Nigeria, which is still strongly Moslem and resistant to change, remains the stronghold of Indirect Rule, and British administrators still play squash with the local Chiefs.

Compared with these courtly, aristocratic leaders, the new African 'upstarts' from the towns have less attraction to most Europeans: all over the continent can be heard the complaints about 'half-baked intellectuals', 'city slickers', 'black Englishmen'. Often the criticism is basically that they are too like Europeans, and that they do not have the 'otherness' which foreigners expect and like in a strange continent, whether Asia or Africa. But it is the city slickers or 'verandah boys', as Nkrumah and his party proudly called themselves, who are becoming the new rulers in most of Africa.

The white man's fascination with tribal Africa

infuriates the detribalized Africans—who have a linger-
ing and sometimes half-justified suspicion that it is
part of a plot to keep Africa primitive and thus subjected. Much of the recent European interest in Africa
has centred on the idea of 'men of two worlds' making
the transition from tribe to town ; a whole succession
of novels by white men about Africans have taken
this theme. Europeans are much more interested in
tribal Africa than educated Africans are : and to some
extent the story of the 'man of two worlds' is perhaps
a dark allegory of the white man's own atavistic desire
for roots and stability. Some of the White attitudes to
the old Africa, particularly in South Africa, are very
sentimental and unrealistic—about a life which is bleak,
fear-ridden and hideously poor. Only the most sophisticated Africans of all, who have been removed from tribal
life long enough to grow fond of it, share this nostalgia.

But the conflict between past and future, Chiefs and
cities, remains a real one for Africans, and many of
them have vividly described their predicament. The
two pulls working on educated Africans could be
illustrated by the careers of two African friends, both
detribalized, who were in London together after the
war : Kwame Nkrumah and Jomo Kenyatta. Nkrumah,
as Premier of Ghana, became one of the strongest
opponents of the power of the Chiefs. Kenyatta, in his
hatred of white domination, became obsessed with the
superiority of the tribal life, which he describes in his
anthropological study of the Kikuyu, *Facing Mount
Kenya*, with the curious and significant dedication :

"To Moigoi and Wamboi and all the dispossessed
youth of Africa : for perpetuation of communion

with ancestral spirits through the fight for African
Freedom, and in the firm faith that the dead, the
living, and the unborn will unite to rebuild the
destroyed shrines."

His obsession led to his encouragement of the Mau
Mau rebellion in Kenya, and his own imprisonment.
The South African coloured novelist Peter Abrahams,
a friend of both men, has vividly described the hell of
the detribalized African in white-dominated states,
who is cut off both from his past and from Western
culture, denouncing the West in excellent English—
a man, not of two worlds, but of none.[1]

Except in a few strong monarchical states, such as
Baganda or Basutoland, the power of the chiefs is now
rapidly waning. The aristocracy of the Chiefs is being
superseded in part by the 'new élite', of the Western-
educated Africans. The rapid creation of this new class
is a remarkable sociological process. Though in some
chiefly strongholds the intelligentsia are from noble
families, in the majority of Africa they are selected by
brains and ability rather than blood: they are in fact
a genuine 'meritocracy'. They are a minority even
smaller than the White 'two percent' whom they are
succeeding. In the whole of English-speaking Africa,
with about eighty million, less than 1 per cent have
been to secondary schools, of whom nearly half are in
South Africa. Although this figure is rapidly rising
with the present plans for mass education, it is well
below the level needed. "Countries in our state of
development", said Professor Arthur Lewis, when

[1] Peter Abrahams: 'Conflict of Culture in Africa', *International
Affairs*, July 1954.

acting as economic adviser to the Ghana government, "are not self-sufficient in secondary school products until about 4 per cent of each generation is entering secondary schools."[1] In university education, Africa is even barer: apart from South Africa, where black education is threatened with special tribal curricula, there are only 3,600 English-speaking Africans at universities or higher technical institutions.

How far this élite will be in control of the Africa of the future, or how far they will be side-stepped by demagogues with the 'common touch', is still an open question. Under colonial rule, education was the key to African advancement and promotion, and the passion for education, degrees and doctorates remains a strong feature of Africans. But there is a danger that the intellectuals will find themselves politically powerless and isolated from their people: 'mad with higher education', as a Basuto proverb says.

The optimism and earnestness of the new Africa is closely connected with the previous sense of African inferiority. That Africans are *not* inferior to Europeans is now generally accepted, proved both by biological evidence and by the achievement of African individuals. But two factors have given Africans a stronger feeling of inadequacy than the other ex-colonial peoples: the institution of slavery, under both Arabs and Europeans, in which the de-humanization of twenty million Africans led foreigners to believe that Africans were sub-human: and the lack of African history.

History is a vital commodity in Africa, fraught with politics. Until very recently it has been assumed that

[1] Letter to *The Economist*, January 10, 1959.

Africa was a totally 'dark continent' before the Europeans arrived—supported by the evidence of nineteenth-century explorers, and the absence of such simple devices as the wheel in East or Central Africa. The 'tsetse-fly belt' which runs across the waist of Africa had acted as an effective barrier to conquest and civilization, and the slave trade had often decimated the tribes, and wrecked their social systems. The European picture of the African as a primitive, helpless person, incapable of civilized behaviour, penetrated deep into the African mind.

But in the last few years, simultaneously with the rise of African pride, there has been the beginnings of a new view of African history. The 'dark ages' of Africa in the eighteenth and nineteenth centuries have obscured much of an earlier civilization : and recent archaeology and historical research have suggested that quite complex African civilizations did exist. The ruins on the East African coast of Kenya and Tanganyika are thought by the most recent authority, Gervase Mathew, to be the work not of Arabs or Persian colonists, but of African Kings. The Yoruba Kingdoms of what is now Nigeria were ordered and well-developed civilizations, which produced the magnificent sixteenth-century bronzes of Benin.

The ruins of Zimbabwe, the mysterious and massive fortress in Southern Rhodesia, have been a special bone of contention between Africans and Europeans, and between left-wing and right-wing observers—the latter claiming that Zimbabwe must have been built by Arabs or earlier colonizers. "If you want to do us a service", an African said to a British journalist in Rhodesia, "find out that Zimbabwe was built by

Africans."[1] It now seems likely that Zimbabwe was in fact the capital of an ancient African kingdom, built perhaps as recently as the sixteenth century. It is easy to exaggerate these indications, but their political import is obvious. "At a time when European mariners had yet to reach the Indian Ocean, or even the Bight of Benin, the kings and counsellors of Central Africa were eating from Chinese porcelain, and when Mr. Strijdoms's forebears drove their ox-carts into the old Transvaal, they encountered men and women who were not at the beginning of a long period of civilized development, but, through times of painful dissolution, were perilously near the end of one."[2]

With all the differences of language, education, tribe, colour and experience, one is tempted to think that Africa is, after all, as disparate as Asia—a conglomeration of peoples who just happen to be inside one land-mass. Certainly up to a few years ago this was the usual view, and all the history of the continent suggests that it has never been a unity : the only people who travelled across it were Arab slave-traders or European explorers : and it was only from them that Negroes could learn that there were other Negroes on the opposite side. The only common factors in the old Africa, apart from its race, were the slave trade, the wildness and incommunicability of the country and the occasional incursions of white men. Ironically, it was only when they were shipped away as slaves that many Negroes must have realized that they were, after all, part of a whole continent of people : and perhaps

[1] Cyril Dunn: *Central African Witness*, Gollancz, 1959.
[2] Basil Davidson: 'The Fact of African History', *Africa South*, March 1958.

it is significant that the first ideas of a black Panafrica
early in this century came from Negroes in the West
Indies and America.

But Africa's potentialities are changing so fast, that
it is now less certain that it may not become a whole,
as it may have been before. For Africans—Negro,
Bantu, English or French—have shown one thing in
common which before the war was scarcely dreamt of:
and that is the sudden surge of self-awareness usually
referred to as African nationalism.

CHAPTER III

NATIONALISM

IT IS AFRICAN NATIONALISM, above all, which is changing the complexion of the continent. There is hardly a territory in Africa where it has not arisen: governments, like the Congo's, who believed they had circumvented it, have been harshly disillusioned. Everyone accepts the existence of the growth: but there is still much uncertainty as to what exactly it *is*. Some people—including Lord Hailey, in his *African Survey* —believe that it should not be called nationalism at all, but 'Africanism', to denote its basically different character. But 'Africanism' is a still more confusing term, which can be used to mean nationalism, the 'African personality', Panafricanism, or (in South Africa) the more extreme wing of nationalism.

What makes African nationalism so different, and so surprising, is the fact that there are hardly any real 'nations' in Africa, in the European or even the Asian sense, to attract a pride of nationhood. Ghana, Nigeria and Kenya did not exist before the twentieth century, and their frontiers—as Africans themselves frequently complain—are the arbitrary creations of British administrators, crossing over tribes, races and mountains.

It is often argued that tribal feeling is still much the strongest force in most of Africa, and that once the first flush of nationhood is over—particularly in West Africa—the new states will soon split up into tribes again, as they were before the white men found them. In view of this fissiparous tendency (a phrase now much in fashion in Africa), there have been serious suggestions that Nigeria should be split up into as many as thirteen autonomous regions. Before Ghana became independent there were very grave doubts as to whether the Ashanti in the north and the Ga and Fanti in the south could keep together. Some African experts believe that the eventual solution for African peace lies in 'provincial autonomy' within states on a Swiss kind of pattern—not only for Africans, but for white tribes too.

But the fact remains that at present most articulate feeling—with some notable exceptions, such as the Baganda in Uganda or the Ashanti in Ghana—centres round the idea of a nation. However bogus the frontiers may be, the facts of communication and administration very soon make Africans aware of their shape and size. It is extraordinary how quickly the creation by Whites of new nations has stimulated Africans to the idea, if not the practice, of nationalism. The formation of the Union of South Africa in 1910, out of two Afrikaner republics and two British colonies, was followed only two years later by the foundation of the African National Congress to unite Africans throughout the Union—the first national, if not nationalistic, African movement in the continent. Somewhat differently, the imposition of the Federation of Central Africa in 1953 has greatly stimulated the Nyasaland African Congress to a sense of nationhood—in this case united against the Federation.

Another unique feature of African nationalism connected with the lack of nations is the lack of a past. Few Africans have a past in which they take much pride, and the difficulties of nationalist leaders are increased by the fact that they are usually rebelling not only against the colonial powers, but also against African chiefs, who are generally very much part of what history there is. In spite of the recent historical discoveries, it remains true that Africans cannot look back to their ancestors with the same confidence and nostalgia as Indians, Chinese or Arabs : and this lack of a heritage has contributed to their uncertainty about their own capacities. Nowhere is this more true than in South Africa, where Africans are both much more aware of the advantages of the Western way of life, and more insistently told about their own barbarous origins.

This turning away from history may have given Africans a worrying lack of stable tradition : but it may also, as in modern Germany or Australia, give them in the future a freedom and flexibility which the older nations lack.

Faced with this lack of ancestors, nationalist leaders have tended to refer vaguely to 'our Glorious African Heritage' without going into too much detail. The eleventh-century civilization of Ghana is thought to have lain about two thousand miles away from the modern Ghana (Guinea)—which was re-named after it on the day of its independence. But the romanticization of ancient Ghana played a useful part in Gold Coast politics, and in national pride. In July 1953, Dr. Nkrumah said :

"In the very early days of the Christian era, long before England had assumed any importance, long even before her people had united into a nation, our ancestors had attained a great empire, which

lasted until the eleventh century, when it fell before
the attacks of the Moors of the North. At its height,
that empire stretched from Timbuktu to Bamako,
and even as far as to the Atlantic. It is said that
lawyers and scholars were much respected in that
empire, and that the inhabitants of Ghana wore gar-
ments of wool, cotton, silk and velvet. There was
trade in copper, gold and textile fabrics, and jewels
and weapons of gold and silver were carried. . . .

"Thus may we take pride in the name of Ghana,
not out of romanticism, but as an inspiration for
the future. . . ."

Ghana nationalism has been helped, not only by this
vague historical vision, but also by the more real inheritance of Ghana national dress, foods and customs
which have never been rejected and which have acted,
as in Asia, as part of the panoply of national conscious-
ness.

But much of the romanticization of Africa's past,
and the vision of her glorious future, came from abroad
—and particularly from America. Sixty years ago
American Negroes were more enthusiastic about their
African connection than they are now, having become
more assimilated into white America. At the end of
the last century, uprooted and bewildered, Negroes in
the Northern States searched for an African lore in
which they could take pride. They found it in such
bodies as the American Methodist Episcopal Church,
which had important connections with the 'Ethiopian'
Church movement which was growing up—with some
of the same causes—in South Africa in the 1880's.
The attraction of Ethiopia lay partly in the Bible, and

the prophetic cry of 'Ethiopia shall stretch out her hands unto God' : and partly in the fact that modern Abyssinia, after the heroic victory over the Italians at Adowa in 1896, became the only independent black state in the continent—in which role it continued to be a brave symbol for Black Africa, until its defeat by Mussolini in 1936.

Some of this new American Negro pride filtered through to Africa and had its effect, for instance, on the Nyasa rising of 1915, organized by John Chilembwe, better known as John Buchan's 'Prester John' ; or on Bantu agitation in the Transkei in South Africa. But a more spectacular impetus was given by a bizarre and unscrupulous Negro Jamaican demagogue, Marcus Aurelius Garvey, who in 1920 founded a 'Negro Empire' in New York, and pledged himself to regain Africa for the black people. With the slogans 'Wake up, Ethiopia !', 'Wake up, Africa !', he founded 'The Universal Negro Improvement and African Communities League'. He appointed himself as President of Africa, and created a Negro nobility, including a Duke of the Nile, Earl of the Congo and Viscount of the Niger. He achieved a very large membership and bought ships, which proved to be unseaworthy, to carry Negroes back to Africa. His project ended in financial disaster, and he spent the end of his life addressing small crowds in Hyde Park : but his movement, preposterous and egotistic though it was, penetrated quite deeply into Africa, and did help to wake Africans up. In the 1920's, according to the West Indian historian C. L. R. James, "the King of Swaziland knew the names of only two black men in the Western world, Jack Johnson and Marcus Garvey".

Garvey's movement had some resemblance to two much earlier and more practical schemes that had already been achieved—the settlement of American ex-slaves in Liberia, and British ex-slaves in Sierra Leone, both on the West Coast of Africa. Like Garvey's 'Back to Africa', they were motivated by a kind of Black Zionism, rather than African nationalism, and they produced considerable problems in the relations between the ex-slaves, who became a Negro aristocracy, and the unprivileged local Africans.

While Garvey was organizing his gimcrack aristocracy in the 'twenties, liberal notions about Africa, and Marxist ideas of anti-colonialism, were spreading rapidly through the West. J. A. Hobson's book on *Imperialism*, published as long ago as 1902, became the bible of the anti-colonialist movement, and the now familiar clichés of African nationalism were acquired from this and other manuals.

It has become a truism to say that Britain taught Africans to revolt against her. The point at which tribalism became nationalism could be detected when Africans in revolt no longer wished to revert to the tribal *status quo*, but to set up a nation in the Western sense, embodying Western ideals. The first nationalists, in the words of one historian, Dr. Roland Oliver, "were people who, in their very enthusiasm for the things of the West, had idealized them and had seen that Europeans as individuals did not conform to those ideals. They had seen through the European. They had seen him as a hypocrite, conspiring to withhold from the African the good things of the West. . . ."[1]

[1] Roland Oliver: 'Too Cheeky, too Thefty', *Twentieth Century*, April 1959.

When the words 'African nationalism' are used by politicians to conjure up a picture of savage black hordes, it is important to remember that the nationalism originated with European teaching. Africans are still infuriated above all by the humbug of the White man, preaching democracy in Europe, and practising oligarchy in Africa.

Many of the weapons of the African nationalists originated in left-wing London. Partly because the language of anti-colonialism originated with Marxists, nationalism has often been mistaken for Communism : often, indeed, the manifestoes and programmes of African movements have been hardly distinguishable in their tone from Soviet pronouncements. But in their eventual aims and character the African nationalists have shown little resemblance to the Communists. Dr. Nkrumah, who describes himself in his autobiography as 'a non-denominational Christian and a Marxist socialist', was reported by the Watson Commission of 1948 to 'have become imbued with a Communist ideology' : but in his leadership since Ghana's independence he has shown little interest in Russia.

While Britain and other colonial powers were first becoming uneasy and divided about the rights of Imperialism in the 'twenties, in many parts of Africa the first considerable bodies of educated Africans were clubbing together to defend, if not to extend, their rights. The early African movements were mostly gatherings of professional Africans, many of them educated in England; the Aborigines Rights Protection Society founded in the Gold Coast in 1897, the Nigerian National Democratic Party founded in 1923, or the African National Congress founded in South Africa in 1912 all consisted of small bodies of lawyers, teachers or doctors trying to protect their people from white exploitation.

These early African leaders were hardly nationalists in the modern sense, though they did speak in terms of their respective 'African nations'. They were cut off from their people, not only by their education, but by the ability of the white governments to make use of them as instruments of government, either directly or indirectly. Many of the leaders were themselves descendants of Chiefs, or allies of them : and several of them were by no means sure that it would be advantageous to give the vote to the African masses.

In the 'thirties the spread of Marxist ideas, the Abyssinian war, the economic depression and the new pace of international diplomacy were all beginning to forge a new, more radical kind of African leader : but it was not until the Second World War that the notion of African independence became widely recognized. It is significant that some of the most far-reaching British decisions regarding Africa were made at the height of the war. The Colonial Development and Welfare Act, which permitted far greater funds to be devoted to the Colonies, was passed during the Battle of Britain : the Atlantic Charter signed by Churchill and Roosevelt in 1941 first laid down the central principle of self-determination, and established 'the right of all people to choose the form of government under which they may live'. Though it may have been forgotten in Britain, the Charter was certainly not unnoticed in Africa : it gave the green light to nationalism. Dr. Azikiwe in Nigeria produced in 1943 a memorandum called 'The Atlantic Charter and British West Africa', which demanded immediate reforms and representative government in West Africa. Even in South Africa Dr. Xuma, the then President of the African National Congress, produced in 1943 a document called 'African Claims', which took as its starting-point the third article of the Atlantic Charter. The new African militancy had further encouragement from America, where there was a strong feeling that the war should not be fought in defence of colonies, and where the Atlantic Charter and its consequences were taken very seriously. All the anti-fascist idealism of the war, which culminated in the United Nations Charter of 1945, gave support to African demands; and the Africans were made very much aware of it by their own participation in the war.

It was the war which was responsible for the first crop of serious nationalist movements, which followed each other with astonishing speed. The United Gold Coast Convention was set up by Dr. Danquah in 1947: in the same year the Kenya African Union held its first Congress in Nairobi. In 1948 Dr. Awolowo set up the 'Action Group' in Western Nigeria, as a rival to Dr. Azikiwe's 'National Council of Nigeria and the Cameroons', founded five years earlier. In 1949 the 'old guard' of the African National Congress in South Africa was outvoted in favour of younger, more radical leaders under Dr. Moroka, committed to demands for an immediate universal franchise. In 1948 the Northern Rhodesian African National Congress was created from a federation of welfare societies, with Godwin Lewanika, the descendant of King Lewanika, as its president.

In the meantime the massive block of French Africa, which had played a crucial role in fighting with the Free French, had also been stirred to much louder demands, encouraged by communists and by the tradition of war-time resistance. In 1946 a mammoth conference of French Black Africa was held at Bamako, on the Niger River, which was the source of most subsequent French African developments: it was there that the Rassemblement Democratique Africain, in its day the biggest mass movement in Africa, was founded by Felix Houphouet-Boigny. In two years it achieved a membership of 700,000; but its alliance with the French Communist Party brought it into increasing difficulties until it eventually split from them in 1950.

Some of these first post-war African movements were genuinely radical bodies, uncompromisingly critical of the régimes and demanding immediate self-government: with modern methods of organization, newspapers, slogans and rallies they quickly built up a mass following. But others were still cautious and middle-class in their demands, and as a result were easily outbidden by more radical rivals. The United Gold Coast Convention was very soon ousted by Nkrumah's Convention People's Party, which countered the demand for self-government with the insistence on self-government *now*. In Northern Rhodesia the chiefly, cautious leadership of Godwin Lewanika was soon succeeded by the more demagogic and uncompromising attack of Harry Nkumbula, who took over as President of the Congress in 1951.

Though the roots of nationalism are many, it has often been economic grievances which have hastened the popular movement. Cocoa disease in Ghana, cotton troubles in Uganda, a copper slump in the Congo, have each lit the fuse of mass discontent.

Whenever a nationalist movement springs up in Africa, it is usual for the local Europeans to take up the cry of 'communism', which is then echoed abroad. The confusion between the two, between Black and Red, is common and often calculated, particularly in South Africa and Rhodesia, to enlist world support against the nationalists. Nearly every African movement from Ghana to South Africa has at one time been branded as communist: but apart from the visits of a few African leaders to Moscow, little evidence has been produced of communist connections. Between Africa and Russia there is very little natural sympathy. The Russian African experts argue that African communities do not yet have the social organization to produce a communist revolution: the Africans on their side are largely preoccupied with their bourgeois revolution, and the few who are invited behind the Iron Curtain are usually more impressed by Pekin than Moscow. African movements have had little need of encouragement from Moscow or from Cairo. "If we confuse nationalism with communism", wrote the former Governor of Uganda, Sir Andrew Cohen, "we are doing a most harmful thing, because successful co-operation with nationalism is our greatest bulwark against communism in Africa."[1]

The nationalist movements have varied a great deal: there has been a basic difference between the West African nationalists, whose fight was relatively an easy one, and who had some kind of continuous tribal

[1] Sir Andrew Cohen: *British Policy in Changing Africa*, Routledge, 1959.

tradition, and the African leaders in the East and South who were confronted with a white settler population —who constituted not only a firmer opposition, but also a greater counter-attraction and potential diversion from nationalism. In general, it has been where the fight has been easiest—in West Africa—that the shouting has been loudest; the West African leaders are often reproving those in the East and South for their lack of militancy, while the Southern leaders accuse the West Africans of bluster and boasting.

Certainly there has been an element of shadow-boxing and play-acting in West African nationalism: the fight was easier than it looked. Since 1948, under either a Labour or a Conservative Government, there has not been much doubt about the future independence of West Africa, though there has been argument about the dates of independence. Long after he had reached agreement with Britain and friendship with the Governor, Nkrumah felt himself impelled, in order to maintain national unity and enthusiasm, to attack the 'imperialists' as if they were unyielding tyrants.

It is this easy victory that has given rise to a common complaint about African nationalism. On the analogy that nations, like individuals, need suffering to integrate their character, the new African states have had a relatively easy beginning compared to Asian or European nations. Among Indian leaders, Nkrumah's references to his struggle do not evoke much sympathy: certainly there can be no comparison between Nehru's lifetime of austere dedication to India and Nkrumah's cheerful ride to national leadership. Many people maintain that the disunity and irresponsibility in Ghana is the result of too quick and effortless a fight for

independence : but the corollary, that in order to forge
sober and unified nations, the colonial powers should
have held on longer, is difficult to argue.

In any case, these walkover victories have by no
means occurred all over Africa ; and in the countries
with a considerable population of white settlers, as the
next chapter will show, the African situation has been
fundamentally different.

CHAPTER IV

SETTLERS

THERE IS NO serious problem, once the principle of self-determination has been granted, about the parts of Africa which are wholly Black : 'the African problem' really refers only to the parts of Africa with white settlers who regard Africa as their home, and who wish to maintain a European way of life. It is, as Africans are never tired of pointing out, a problem, not of Africans, but of Europeans.

It is an often-quoted law of Africa that 'the greater the proportion of Whites, the greater the problem'. In the whole continent there are only five million white people, or $2\frac{1}{2}$ per cent of the whole population : and most of them are concentrated at the extreme north and south of the continent, the regions which have the most congenial climate, and the greatest wealth. South Africa and Algeria have much the largest number of white settlers : South Africa with three million Whites out of fourteen million, Algeria with one and a half million Whites out of nine million. It is in those two countries, similar in many ways, where white governments and institutions are most firmly entrenched, and therefore that the clash is most dangerous. Though Algeria is part of the Arab world, and therefore outside the scope of this book, the prolonged war between French settlers and Arab nationalists has an obvious significance for the rest of Africa.

A 'colour spectrum' of Africa could be compiled to

show the diminishing proportions of Whites, varying roughly according to the comfort and climate of the country, with South Africa at one extreme and Nigeria at the other :

 1. South Africa . . . . 1 in 4
 2. (Algeria) . . . . 1 „ 9
 3. Southern Rhodesia . . 1 „ 13
 4. Northern Rhodesia . . 1 „ 41
 5. Angola . . . . 1 „ 47
 6. Mozambique . . . 1 „ 119
 7. Kenya . . . . 1 „ 136
 8. Belgian Congo . . . 1 „ 200
 9. French Equatorial Africa . 1 „ 225
10. French West Africa . . 1 „ 270
11. Tanganyika . . . . 1 „ 390
12. Nyasaland . . . . 1 „ 511
13. Ghana . . . . 1 „ 662
14. Uganda . . . . 1 „ 700
15. Nigeria . . . . 1 „ 2,700

But at the black end of the spectrum, the 'problem' ceases to be serious, because the Whites do not regard the country as their home. In the Congo or Uganda, for instance, the European residents have never supposed that they could establish themselves indefinitely. The problem is proportionate not so much to white numbers as to white land. Land, which is prized by Africans even more than by Europeans, is the crucial factor : for it brings with it stability, confidence and power. It is in South Africa, Algeria, Central Africa and Kenya that the dispute over land is more serious : and it is in South Africa, where 89 per cent of the country is owned by the white 21 per cent of the population, that the situation is most bitter of all.

With settlers comes the colour bar, and all that it entails. The difference between a country with white settlers (like Kenya) and a neighbouring state with only a white community (like Uganda) is immediately recognizable. Hotels, bars, restaurants and cinemas are for Whites only, and Africans live in townships or 'locations'—a unique product of Africa, the segregated, fenced-off settlements of shacks and cheap brick houses, strictly supervised by the police. Africans come into the 'white town' only on certain terms, and often only with special passes. Though some white cities, such as Nairobi or Leopoldville, are gradually relaxing their social colour bar, the appearance of these segregated cities is curiously uniform. Because the city centres are always white, and used much more by cars than by pedestrians, they can look oddly lifeless and artificial. White cities, and their periphery of locations, stretch from Leopoldville in the Congo down through the copper-belt of the Congo and Rhodesia, to Southern Rhodesia and South Africa.

Around the white settlers has accumulated all the paraphernalia and myth of white supremacy : the arguments, biblical, pseudo-scientific or historical, that the races were not meant to mix, and the whole vocabulary of phrases to indicate superiority and the white man's burden : 'Christian trusteeship', 'civilizing mission', 'sacred trust', 'natives have the mental age of ten', 'it's taken us two thousand years to get where we are : how can they expect to get there in twenty?' To this a typical African reply is : "What is it they're defending? Two thousand years of war !"

In some of the 'multi-racial' states of Africa, the position is complicated by the presence of other minorities, who stand as awkward buffers between black and white. In Kenya there are three times as many Indians as Whites, and some observers believe the eventual problem will be the Indian one. In Durban in South Africa there are more Indians than Africans, and Cape Town has a majority of Coloureds (half-castes). But the central problem, round which the others revolve, remains a white one.

The existence of five million white settlers in Africa threatens to become—if it is not already—one of the most embarrassing problems of the West. It is easy to maintain in theory that a minority of $2\frac{1}{2}$ per cent should not be allowed to interfere with the ambitions and rights of the other $97\frac{1}{2}$: but the white minorities still have a strong hold on the loyalties of the West, for it is they who have largely developed the continent. Their beginnings, at a time when few people were concerned with self-determination or the rights of Africans, have the courage and hardihood associated with all colonizers. Settlers like to remind their American and Australian critics of how they treated *their* indigenous people.

Who are settlers? Recently the word has come to be used as if they were an entirely different race of people from the Europeans : and certainly, though they mostly originated in Europe, they very soon develop characteristics, not only towards Africans, but towards other Europeans, which make them appear distinctly foreign. But there are two kinds of settler. The first are the landowners, usually farmers, who have staked their wealth on the African land. There are relatively

few of them. Out of a white population of forty-two
thousand in Kenya, only about four thousand are
thought to be agricultural landowners ; while in South
Africa, out of three millions, only about one hundred
thousand own farms. The landowners arouse resentment out of proportion to their small numbers, and
whenever there is a major African agitation it is mainly
directed against 'the men who took our land'.

The remaining settlers are the great majority whose
stake in Africa is their job rather than their land. Their
status varies enormously : in Kenya, the most aristocratic white settlement—except, perhaps, the Kivu district of the Congo—most of the trade, clerical work
and artisan's jobs are left to the Africans or Indians.
In South Africa and Rhodesia there is a large white
proletariat, who demand protection from the competition of African workers, and therefore complicate the
problem. But in no part of Africa are there white
house-servants, white dustmen, road-menders, gar-
deners or heavy manual workers of any kind. Heavy
work is regarded as 'natives' work' or 'kaffirs' work' :
it is a common sight in South Africa to see a white
postman with a black assistant following with the postman's burden. A surprising aspect of Europe, to a
white South African visiting for the first time, is the
sight of white men doing 'kaffirs' work'.

This is one factor which makes settlers special : they
are in one sense aristocrats. Their whole conception of
Africa, ever since the first explorers marched through
the jungle with a line of bearers, has depended on
white leadership—a domination of a more personal
kind than the British in India or Ceylon, who returned
to Britain at the end of their lives. But together with

this traditional domination is a growing feeling of uncertainty and fear of the African majority. It is this mixture of supremacy and fear which can make settlers awkward. From this comes the popular picture of 'The Settler'—the bullying, eccentric *bwana* or *baas*, commanding black servants with wild intolerance, spluttering about communists and Fabians in England, and living a life of idle leisure reminiscent of England in the 'twenties.

The insulation of these white societies against the rest of Africa and the world is something which strikes the visitor immediately. The white population of Kenya is less than that of Surbiton, and in the whole of the Central African Federation there are fewer white people than in Newcastle: but even the smallest white towns produce a way of life which is cut off and largely unaware of the remaining population. The very word 'population' is usually taken to mean 'white population', and to mention the total figure is often to be taken for a 'liberal'.

In this restricted circle it is easy to forget the extraordinary premises of daily existence. The network of discriminatory laws against the Africans, the allocation of land, the constant discipline of the police or the Native Affairs departments, and the whole elaborate machinery which was constructed to ensure the white man's safety and privileges, are hardly visible to the normal European resident. It is quite possible, as it was in Victorian England, to believe that acts of charity and consideration to servants can compensate for the hardships of the working classes. The fact that the whole system has been devised for the benefit of Whites is not easily remembered.

But the unusual attitudes of the settler, odd as it seems to the visitor, is not necessarily the result of a long stay in Africa: one of the strangest features of the continent is how quickly it changes people. Left-wing labourers emigrating to Rhodesia can change in a few years to champions of white supremacy, both in politics and private lives—often becoming more extreme than born settlers. Much of the leadership of the right-wing Dominion Party in Rhodesia comes from English immigrants; and American, English or Jewish arrivals in South Africa soon conform to orthodox South African attitudes. The 'liberal' sector of white South Africa comes mainly from South Africans of the second or third generation, not from the newcomers. It is a powerful argument of the settlers, that immigrants who arrive from Europe full of criticisms and idealism change their minds when they see the local situation.

All the logic of world history seems to dwindle in Africa, before the overwhelming pressures—the continuing challenge of a continent waiting to be opened up, the sense of confusions and chaos beyond the borders of white life, and the cushioning from harsh politics which is always provided by willing servants and friendly paternalism. "*My* servants are quite happy" "Think what these natives' lives were like before the white men came": "Can you seriously imagine those people running the country?"—these are the arguments which so easily demoralize the liberal immigrant, or even some African political leaders. For the feeling that Africa is a malign and savage continent, waiting to take back the land into chaos, is a feeling which haunts both Whites and Blacks—and which can easily be made to justify stern measures, in Ghana as in South Africa.

But mixed with the more rational justifications of white supremacy, there are others more emotional, and perhaps therefore more dangerous. A great deal has been written recently about the subconscious fears that lie beneath the famous settlers' shibboleth, which stretches from Kenya to Kentucky: "Would you like your daughter to marry a black man?" That question, which seems to spring up in some form at nearly every white political meeting in Africa, sums up much of the white settlers' irrational fear. The question presupposes three significant assumptions: first, that African advancement must entail more miscegenation; second, that white daughters will *want* to marry black men; third, that such mixed marriages would be not only disgusting, but disastrous.

The fears behind this question are part of the broad subject of racial prejudice, which is not confined to Africa. Sexual feelings play a considerable part in racial attitudes in Africa. This is shown both by the evidence of sexual relations in the past—including the presence of a million half-castes, compared to three million whites, in South Africa; and by the present harshness of the laws against mixed marriages and miscegenation. In South Africa the enforced sentence for miscegenation is six months' imprisonment. In Southern Rhodesia, an African who married a Dutch girl could only live on a mission farm. Even in the University at Salisbury, regarded as the bastion of liberalism in Central Africa, an African lecturer could not be appointed after he had married a Canadian.

The combination of harsh laws with quite frequent infringement seems to suggest that settlers are not as averse to miscegenation as they would like to be. The guilt and repression which results, and its play on politics, has been the theme of several studies and novels—most notably Alan Paton's story of an erring Afrikaner policeman, *Too Late the Phalarope*. In a provocative study of race relations in Madagascar, called *Prospero and Caliban*, a French psychologist, O. Mannoni, has suggested that settlers are subject to the 'Prospero complex', in which they are preoccupied by the desire to dominate, but also fascinated by the animal lusts which the 'natives' (Caliban) seem to represent. The behaviour of Prospero, domineering, paternalistic, and irrational, very ambivalent in his attitude to Caliban and Ariel, is full of resemblances to the white men in Africa.

The fear of miscegenation and a 'coffee-coloured nation', mixed with the more straightforward fear of black supremacy and the loss of white privileges, have forced settlers into their lonely stand against African nationalism. Their case for support is a plausible one: they have developed the continent, brought to it wealth and industry, and staked their future on it. But however comprehensible, the stand of the settlers remains acutely dangerous, both for themselves and for the West. So long as white minorities rule over Africa, the attitude of all white men is suspect: the support to white supremacy given by Britain and America associates the West with the colour bar, against the apparently non-racial policies of the East. The more Africa becomes 'polarized' into independent black states in the West and East, and white-ruled states in the North and South, the more difficult it becomes for the world outside to sit on the fence: and between 195 million Africans and 5 million Europeans, there can be only one eventual outcome.

CHAPTER V

LIBERALS

Between the two poles of African nationalism and white supremacy in the multi-racial territories, lies the small body of people known as 'liberals': meaning Whites who believe in granting increasing political rights to Africans.

The term is vague. Nearly every white politician has at one time described himself as a liberal, and it can mean no more than being friendly to Africans—in their place. It is common for white leaders to say in private: "I'm something of a liberal myself, you know: but I've got to go slowly, to carry my voters with me"—so that visitors are sometimes given the odd impression that white Africa consists entirely of leftward-looking people, who happen by some mutual misunderstanding to be marching right.

There are all degrees of so-called liberals, from the Afrikaner nationalist in South Africa who believes that white farmers should stop flogging natives, to the radical who believes that the only solution lies in joining an African nationalist movement, to 'liberalize it' from within. The word does not have much connection with Gladstone or free trade: but it does have some parallel with the position of the Liberal Party in the 'twenties and 'thirties in Britain. Liberals in Africa often stand in their attitude to African nationalism much as the Liberal Party in Britain stood towards the Labour Party: they believe that a compromise is possible between nationalism and white supremacy, and that they, as liberals, can lead Africans away from their militant stand—as the British Liberals hoped, and still hope, to lead the working-class voters away from trade-union tyranny and class feeling. Just as some English Liberals decided that their position was unrealistic and impotent, and preferred to join the Labour Party and thus influence it, so a very few Whites in Africa have joined forces with African political movements.

But while it is true that at times nearly every white man in Africa *sounds* like a liberal, it is also true that, in the English sense, hardly anyone *is*—at least to the extent of supporting universal suffrage. Only in South Africa, where Africans have no votes at all, and where therefore the prospects of improvement are distant, does the Liberal Party advocate 'one man, one vote'. Liberals usually abhor African nationalism, or 'black supremacy' as they sometimes call it, as much as white supremacy, and it is axiomatic in their policy that some kind of compromise can be achieved between the two. Many liberals argue that if Africans were to worry less about their political rights and votes, and were to concentrate on education, welfare and economic improvements, they would gain far more than they would lose. Once they had achieved civilized standards, the whites would yield their power more willingly and peacefully.

This theory of 'schools, not votes', was first put forward by Booker T. Washington, the Negro leader in America in the 1910's, who began his life in slavery and rose with the help of white philanthropists to be principal of the large Negro technical institute in Tuskegee, Alabama. The Booker Policy was popularized in Africa by his West African protégé, James Aggrey, the great educationalist at Achimota in the Gold Coast. The idea was welcomed in South Africa during the 'twenties, both among Whites and African intellectuals : and it is still much advocated by white liberals —particularly in Rhodesia. But now a more militant spirit has caught up the African leaders, who are much more inclined to follow Nkrumah's precept, engraved below his effigy in Accra : "Seek ye first the political kingdom, and the rest will be added thereto."

In their desire to avoid African domination, and to safeguard the future of the white minority, liberals have devised various electoral schemes, or 'fancy franchises', which give some kind of loading to the white voter, or different forms of 'cross-voting' between the races. Behind these schemes is the idea that, by giving limited numbers of Africans the vote, or by giving all Africans a limited vote, the pressure behind African nationalism can be gradually diverted, until eventually racial politics will disappear altogether, and candidates of all races will be elected by voters of all races.

One of the most vocal liberal organizations in the past has been the Capricorn Africa Society, which was first set up in 1952 by a persuasive Scots idealist, Colonel David Stirling, to advocate among other things the Central African Federation ; and which has since, in a rather altered form, set up branches in territories of East and Central Africa. It has been the view of Capricorn that the only salvation for the multi-racial territories is for all races to adopt a 'common African patriotism', and that both Africans and Europeans should abandon their racial strongholds in favour of a raceless organization where white minorities would be protected by a system of multiple votes.

The Capricorn ideal achieved some impressive support among white settlers in Rhodesia and Kenya, and even among Africans in areas where African organizations themselves were young. In its attacks on social segregation and on the extremes of white supremacy, it certainly served to improve race relations. But in its attempt to provide a substitute both for white supremacy and for black nationalism, it has so far failed: and it has probably failed largely because of the intrinsic weakness of liberalism in Africa—that it has no source of political power. The appeal to white voters, that by compromising with Africans they can ensure their quiescence, does not carry weight among an electorate obsessed with immediate fear of the African majority: while the appeal to Africans, that by abandoning nationalism they can become part of a much broader society, does not carry conviction among people who have set up nationalist movements as a defence against white supremacy. The appeal to Africans to 'drop your racial weapons' while Whites remain entrenched in their constitutional castle, is open to obvious criticisms.

The white liberals, caught between the whirlpool of white supremacy and the grinding rocks of black nationalism, are in a lonely situation in Africa, unwelcome on either side. To the advocates of white supremacy they are ineffectual trouble-makers, rocking the boat; while to most Africans they appear to be trying to impose white leadership on to black power.

This is the main complaint of political Africans against white liberals: that they assume that Africans cannot lead themselves. Once African pride is involved in a militant political movement, the idea of following Whites is immediately suspect—and only those Europeans, like Trevor Huddleston or Michael Scott, who identify themselves entirely with the movement are accepted as leaders.

The militant Africans' dislike of liberals is a fact often used by supporters of white supremacy as an argument in favour of the *status quo*. "Give us Verwoerd—then we know where we are": "Now that Todd's out of the way we can get organized"—these are common arguments against liberals, or even against the scarcely-liberal United Party in South Africa. This anti-liberalism does not imply any acquiescence in the régimes of Verwoerd or Welensky, but rests on the fear that liberals will divert Africans from an all-out assault on white supremacy. The 'give us Verwoerd' line is not always entirely honest: many quite militant Africans in South Africa in private long for the return of the United Party, and have friendly relations with white liberals. But it is as politically dangerous for an African to have openly cordial relations with liberals as it is for a white political leader to have visible friendships with Africans. It is a corollary which is not perhaps always understood: the same white politician who will say, "of course I'm a liberal, but I can't afford to show it in public . . ." will speak with bitter uncomprehension of African leaders—like Tom Mboya in Kenya or Azikiwe in Nigeria—who have spoken privately in favour of whites, but publicly attack them.

Stronger than their dislike for white liberals, is the militant Africans' antagonism to the Africans who collaborate with them, or with the white government as a whole. The words 'Quisling', 'stooge', 'collaborator', 'traitor', 'sell-out', 'Uncle Tom', 'Capricorn', 'white man's boy', are heard all the way from Nairobi to Cape Town. It is a situation by no means confined to Africans, and much of the jargon is borrowed from the wartime resistance in Europe. But for Africans who are unconfident of their own resources and culture, and are easily deflected by white charms, it is a particularly bitter division.

The derogatory phrase 'Uncle Tom', fashionable in both Africa and America, expresses the African dislike for the sentimental picture popularized by Harriet Beecher Stowe, of the faithful, uncomplaining Negro servant, unembittered by his humiliation and beloved of Whites. The more the opportunities for 'collaboration', the more bitter the conflict is likely to be. In Kenya, Central Africa, or in Ghana before independence, where 'moderate' Africans served in the Government, while the more militant preferred to stay out, the division between 'quislings' and 'resistance' has been sharp. It is specially sharp in territories, such as Northern and Southern Rhodesia, where African representatives are elected to parliament by voters who are predominantly White—and who are therefore made to appear as African leaders, when they are in fact regarded as 'quislings'. The presence of African M.P.s in parliament, who are not elected by Africans, has made the African hostility to recent constitutional changes in Rhodesia particularly fierce.

In Nyasaland, a proud nationalistic territory intent on seceding from the Central African Federation, the attitude to Africans collaborating with the Federal Parliament is much more bitter: a former President of the Nyasa Congress, Manoah Chirwa, who remained a member of the Federal Parliament after he had been called on to resign, and retained close friendships with white liberals, was in consequence angrily attacked as being 'too fond of tea'.

'Too fond of tea' expresses much of the awkwardness between the African leader and the white liberal: the tea-party in the white drawing-room, with delicate plates balanced on the knee, is often taken by Africans as a symbol of white wiles. The liberal drawing-room is a difficult frontier, both politically and psychologically. On the one hand, the educated African, resenting the slightest hint of white patronizing or paternalism, touchy on matters of racial pride, and often finding a slight where none was intended: on the other hand, the white liberal, determined to show himself different from other whites, sometimes activated as much by a sense of guilt as expediency, and anxiously trying to please or agree. Africans between themselves are always full of half-mocking stories about encounters with liberals. This is part of an African dialogue I recorded in Johannesburg:

"Have you ever been to a party, or to dinner at one of those swank suburban white homes where the host is very particular how to address you? Yes, I went to a house where the hostess said to me, 'I'm going to give you a kind of food, it's very troublesome to eat.' Look, Louis, if a man is crawling on his knees to be nice to me, it only means one of two things—that he's trying to be nice to me because I'm black, or he's trying to get something out of me. I don't want anybody to like me because I am black."

Some of this criticism comes probably from linger-ing African feelings of inferiority, from the difficult aftermath of a teacher-pupil, father-son relationship : but some of it may reflect unreality in many liberals' attitude. For, while liberals are often suggesting that if only misunderstandings and suspicions could be re-moved, and racial prejudices forgotten, Whites and Blacks could work together for a happy multi-racial state; the fact remains that the interest of Africans and liberals *are* very different. In every territory in the continent, Africans wish to have the political con-trol to which they feel entitled by their majority. They do not wish to eject Whites, but they wish to run their own country as they think fit.

Liberals on the other hand are apt to be motivated not principally by African interests, but by the desire to ensure the survival of privileged white settlements in Africa. Their arguments are inclined to be two-edged : while they appeal to Africans to work with them for a raceless community, they appeal to other Whites—and particularly white financial backers—on the basis that their policy will ensure the stability of white industry and commerce. Some liberals in South Africa talk openly of assuming the role of Kerenskys, when the present government finds itself incapable of handling the racial conflict : but it is not a role for which Africans can be expected to embrace much en-thusiasm.

The objects of African nationalism and white liberal-ism may not be incompatible : certainly, where white settlement has not been entrenched, as in Ghana, Afri-can control has meant more, not less, white population and even investment. But so long as the basis of a territory remains white governmental control, the first object of the African opposition must be the substitution of African control : and so long as white liberals refuse to join them in this, their interests must be divergent.

It is a common argument of liberals that those who oppose their 'non-racial' solution to Africa, are themselves being racialistic, and assuming that 'all blacks are good, all Whites are bad'. But the divisions between Black and White in colonial Africa are much more than racial divisions : they embody all the classic divisions of class and privilege, with the two sides separated by an enormous and deliberate gulf. In this context, the words 'anti-Black' and 'anti-White' can be gross over-simplifications, and liberals can often deceive themselves as to the extent of their concessions.

CHAPTER VI

BLACKNESS

"FROM NOW ON", said Kwame Nkrumah at the Accra conference in April 1958, "nobody can look down on Africa." At the same conference he mentioned the now-famous phrase, the 'African personality'. "In the last century", he said later, "the Europeans discovered Africa : in the next century the Africans will discover Africa."

What kind of a place will they discover? No one visiting the black parts of the continent can doubt that they will become less comprehensible as they cast off their lines from Europe. The pressure towards 'Africanization' is discernible in every sphere : not only in politics, but in sport, trades unions, writing, art, and most of all religion. Every idea that comes from the West will suffer a sea-change before it is accepted in Africa. Africans often feel that European values should be not so much rejected as purified—producing education without privilege, government without arrogance, technology without inhumanity and above all, Christianity without racialism. With the pressure towards Africanization, Christianity—with its associations of foreignness and white dominations—has already lost ground to Islam, which has no appearance of colour bar, and no connection with Europe. In the new secular schools and colleges of independent Africa, Christianity is no longer regarded as the key to learning and civilization.

Behind the mystique of the 'African personality' lies all the pride of Africa : the belief that Africans will lead the world not by strength, but by force of character : that they, the last continent to mature, will take the best from every other continent, and forge a new civilization finer than any of them : that everything they adopt will be as essentially African as Europe is European. Behind it, too, lies the sense of nothingness in the past—a nothingness deriving from slavery, foreign domination and an obliterated memory. Only in this century has Africa looked at itself in the mirror, and seen itself.

But the image of Africa is still hazy and uncertain : it is in the midst of changes too violent and uprooting to allow any settled 'personality' to show itself. New industrial cities in the South have upset all the social stability, and produced quite new African types—with little apparent connection with their rural cousins : in place of the Chiefs, counsellors and headsmen are black Cockneys, black factoryworkers, and the self-conscious society of the black bourgeoisie.

For most English-speaking Africans, the idea of the 'African personality' is not particularly attractive. They are too anxious to acquire Western skills, degrees and educational equality to bother about blackness : and the glories of the African past, however much they may be plugged by politicians, do not usually excite them.

> "Don't preserve my customs,
> As some fine curios
> To suit some white historian's taste"

wrote the Nigerian poet, Denis Osadebay[1] : and his attitude is reflected in much contemporary black writing—which tends to be in English, rather than in African languages. In South Africa, the desire to escape from the past is even stronger—a fact which I discovered abruptly when editing *Drum*, where the urban Africans, even the highly-educated ones, hated to be reminded of their tribal ancestry : "cut out this junk about kraals and folk-tales and Basutos in blankets", said a typical reader : "give us jazz and film stars, man !" There have been a few writers in West Africa, notably the Ghanaian author Amos Tutuola, author of *The Palm Wine Drunkard*, who have blended folk-tales and modern idioms in a most un-English way. But their works appeal more to English readers than to African, and the more acceptable novels—like Cyprian Ekwensi's *People of the City*—are more Western and detribalized in character.

But while English-speaking Africans have been escaping from their roots, the intellectual French Africans have had the opposite tendency : they are determined to be black. It is they who first conceived the mystique of the 'African personality', and coined their own word for it, *négritude*—which might be translated as 'the importance of being black'. This dichotomy between the education of French and English Africans is fundamental : while British Africans have been concentrating on political independence, the educated French Africans have also been concerned with cultural independence. The cultured equivalent of the Accra political conferences in 1958, at which English

[1] Quoted, with other examples in this chapter, from 'In Search of an African Personality', by Ulli Beier, *Twentieth Century*, April 1959.

Africans dominated, was the Congress of Black Artists and Writers in Paris in 1957, organized by French Africans and American Negroes, with few English-speaking Africans present. Paris has been the cultural capital of the Continent—though with the loosening of its political hold, French intellectuals have recently turned more to their own countries, and *négritude* has become more Africanized.

The reason for the French interest in *négritude* is paradoxical. The African élite or *évolués* from the French territories have been allowed and encouraged to become part of European society, in a way that English Africans never have. In Paris Africans move far more freely and confidently, with more relaxed attitudes, than they do in London : they have become more assimilated into French society, both in Africa and France, and thus also more cut off from their people.

As the idea of Panafrica was invented by a West Indian in London, so the concept of *négritude* was originated by a West Indian—from Martinique—in Paris. Aimé Césaire, regarded now as one of the major French poets, has described graphically how he became aware of *négritude*. He had been educated at the Sorbonne in Paris, and thoroughly assimilated into French life. One day he found himself embarrassed by sitting in a train next to an ordinary black sailor. Arriving home, he was suddenly appalled by his first re-action : he realized that he had behaved as if he were a Frenchman. He wrote in 1939 a long poem about Martinique called 'Notes on a Return to the Native Country', which has been called the 'manifesto of *négritude*'. It championed the passive greatness of the African :

"*Eia* for those who never invented anything
  Eia for those who never conquered anything
  But who in awe give themselves to the essence of
    things."

After Césaire's discovery, several black writers in
Paris, feeling they had been Frenchified out of existence, determined to be Africans rather than black
Frenchmen. The idea of *négritude* soon spread from
the West Indies to French West Africa, and in doing
so became concerned with Africa as a reality rather
than an ideal. The most distinguished of the African
writers is Léopold-Sédar Senghor, who is now, at 52,
one of the three leading African politicians in French
West Africa. Like his friend Césaire, he was educated
in Paris: he spent twelve years in the French National
Assembly, and helped to frame both the Fourth and
Fifth Republics. But also like Césaire, he has set his
face back to Africa: in his best-known poem, 'New
York', he says:

"New York, I say to you: New York let black blood
    flow into your blood
  That it may rub the rust from your steel joints, like
    an oil of life. . . ."

Outside their poetry, they have discussed endlessly
the place of Africa in the world of the future, largely
in the pages of a remarkable journal published in Paris,
Présence Africaine.
  They believe that Africa has a powerful cultural
character of its own, formed by the common past of
slavery and suffering, and by the communal and self-
less tradition of the tribe. "Culture in our civilization",
said Alioun Diop, the Editor of *Présence Africaine*, at

the Paris Cultural Congress in 1956, "is accessible to all men of goodwill, and is not reserved, as a separate activity or luxurious ornament, for a few privileged people." At the same Congress, Senghor outlined the characteristics of Negro culture. The Negro, he said, is a person with open senses with no obstacles between subject and object : he feels, where the white man sees. "White reason is analytical, by practice : black reason is intuitive, by participation." "The more they are inspired by African culture", Senghor says of African writers, "the more they will raise themselves to international rank : the more they turn their back on Mother Africa, the more they will degenerate and weaken."[1]

Some of this idealization of Africa is very hazy and sentimental, like the feelings of expatriates or rootless intellectuals all over the world. It is also mainly limited to the West Coast, and might more accurately be called the 'West African Personality'. Even more romantic than the French Africans are the American Negroes or West Indians, who are often appalled by Africa when they actually see it, with its filling-stations, juke-boxes and Coca-Cola : poets like Langston Hughes, Robert E. Hayden or Countee Cullen hark back to the Africa which Africans themselves least like :

"What is Africa to me :
Copper sun or scarlet sea,
Jungle star of jungle track,
Strong bronzed men, or regal black. . . ."[2]

[1] L. S. Senghor: 'L'Esprit de la Civilisation ou les lois de la culture négro-africaine', *Présence Africaine*, June-November 1956.
[2] Heritage: from *Color*, by Countee Cullen, Harper & Brothers, 1925.

This vision of Africa does not at all fit in with the mood of modern African nationalism, which is determined above all to have progress and technical skills. When at the Accra conference in December 1958 a group of French Africans tried to pass a resolution about the 'African personality', they met with little sympathy from the English-speaking majority. Nkrumah and his friends want to display an African personality as a rallying cry and a political weapon, but not at the cost of economic advancement.

Many English-speaking African intellectuals are apt to mock the cult of *négritude*:

> "Let pedants tease their pompous heads
> While to my repertoire I add
> (The sound, if not the spirit of)
> Our new-coined
> Intellectuals' slogan—
> Négritude."[1]

As Africa acquires confidence, and builds up a new past of its own, so the gap between the ideal Africa of the poets and the real Africa of the politicians, between the jungle track and the Coca-Cola bottle, may begin to narrow. The uncertainty about the 'African personality' is very much part of the black intellectuals' whole predicament: but in its broadest sense, the expression of a black soul has a boundless and obvious appeal to a people who have been conditioned to seeing themselves as 'only half a man'.

"I say that once Africa is free and independent", Kwame Nkrumah said at the Accra Conference in

---

[1] From '. . . And the Other Immigrant', by Wole Soyinka, *Black Orpheus*, Ibadan, May 1959.

December 1958, "we shall see a flowering of the human spirit second to none. . . . Some of us, I think, need reminding that Africa is a continent on its own. It is not an extension of Europe or any other continent. We want, therefore, to develop our own community and an African personality. Others may feel that they have evolved the very best way of life, but we are not bound, like slavish imitators, to accept it as our mould."

CHAPTER VII

PANAFRICA

At first sight, Africa is the most parochial of continents, with a scarcely detectable connection between its corners. The fact, which John Gunther discovered, that to telephone Ghana from South Africa you are routed through London, is symbolic of all kinds of communication. Meetings, not only between Ghanaians and South Africans, but between Ghanaians and Kenyans or Rhodesians, are much more likely to occur in London than in Africa. The only transport between the East and West, apart from special planes and lorries to Mecca, is an aeroplane of Lebanon airways which flies once a week between Accra and Khartoum. The shortest distance for flying from Kenya to Ghana is through Johannesburg—a fact which causes some embarrassment to African dignitaries.

The practical difficulties of Panafrica were brought home to me forcefully when, editing the African magazine *Drum* in Johannesburg, we first tried to extend the circulation of the magazine to West and East Africa. The ship from Cape Town to Takoradi, in Ghana, on which copies of the magazine were carried, left once every ten weeks, and took a fortnight, if it did not break down, for the voyage. There was no rail or road connection except for a track through the Congo. Nor was there any railway to East Africa : the road journey was occasionally undertaken by strong cars in ten days, but the only feasible method of surface transport was the ship which sailed once a month for Mombasa.

The psychological differences were equally difficult : fundamental misunderstandings existed between our readers in the three corners of the continent. Ghanaians usually believed Johannesburg to be a shanty town, and found difficulty in crediting that it contained African doctors or nurses : they assumed the whole of South Africa to be in a state of open civil war, frequently confusing it with the Mau Mau. Black South Africans, on the other hand, expected Ghanaians to be almost as wealthy and spectacular as Americans, living in an African Eldorado, and were gravely disillusioned by pictures of slums in Lagos as bad as those in Johannesburg.

The overriding impression we gained was that one part of Africa was not, except in the broadest issues, interested in the other parts. The number of features we could include which were of equal interest to all territories was tiny : and as a result the magazine was gradually split up—as it is still—into different editions, each featuring local news.

But it would be rash to generalize from this and other evidence—which is abounding—that Panafrica is a complete myth. A few events have reverberated through the black communities of the continent with a force that seems to have broken all frontiers. One of the first of them was the Abyssinian war of 1935-36, which pushed up the circulations of African newspapers from the Gold Coast to Cape Town. Probably the three most important since the war have been the Mau Mau, the independence of Ghana and the Pan-African Congress in Ghana in 1958. However misunderstood and hazy, these three big, simple events have been grasped everywhere. There is a Mau Mau gang of hooligans in Johannesburg, a gang-leader called Jomo, and the shout of 'Ghana!' was a slogan in the 1957 bus boycott. A cover picture of Dr. Nkrumah, or the words of Mau Mau, could sell copies of *Drum* equally effectively in South, East and West. If Africanism was produced by railways and newspapers, Panafricanism may yet be generated by aeroplanes and cheap radios.

Like African nationalism, Panafricanism—if it really is an -ism—owes much to America and the West Indies, which bears out the saying that 'You never see Africa whole until you're out of it'. The idea of Panafrica was invented by a West Indian barrister in London, Henry Sylvester-Williams, who, after meeting visiting African Chiefs and politicians, decided to call a Panafrica conference in 1900 to protest against the aggression of British imperialists. Thirty delegates met, mostly from Britain and the West Indies, and gained a promise from Queen Victoria, through the Colonial Secretary, Joseph Chamberlain, 'not to overlook the interests and welfare of the native races'. But the movement petered out a few years later, when Sylvester-Williams returned to the West Indies and died.

But the 'Father of Panafricanism' was a bearded Negro intellectual, the fierce and radical Dr. William Du Bois, who has lived to see the beginnings of African independence—though in a much tamer, and more bourgeois way, than he had hoped. He founded the American 'National Association for the Advancement of Coloured People' in 1909, in opposition to the moderate policies of Booker Washington. He soon

took a strong interest in Africa—not, as Marcus
Garvey did, as a receptacle for American Negro ex-
pansion, but as a continent of black people suffering
similar, but more serious, indignities to their American
cousins.

As early as 1914 Du Bois wrote, in his book, *The
Negro* :

> "There is slowly arising not only a curiously
> strong brotherhood of Negro blood throughout the
> world, but the common cause of the darker races
> against the intolerable assumption and insults of
> Europeans has already found expression. Most men
> in the world are coloured. A belief in humanity
> means a belief in coloured men. The future world
> will, in all reasonable possibility, be what coloured
> men make it."

The 'curiously strong brotherhood of Negro blood'
was not, as it happened, to include the bulk of American Negroes : their enthusiasm for Africa at the time of
Garvey soon subsided with the improvement in their
own situation, and most American Negroes preferred
to forget about their kinship with people who they
were inclined to regard as embarrassing savages. Only
a few Negro intellectuals, like Du Bois, were excited
by their relationship to a huge and undeveloped continent. Africa continued to look to America, but
America preferred to look away; the prospect of a
'Negro International' soon changed to the idea of
Panafrica.

Du Bois was responsible for a series of five Panafrican Congresses, from Paris in 1919 to Manchester

in 1945. From the first small gathering of 'American
coloured men in frock coats or business suits, polished
French Negroes who hold public offices, Senegalese
who sit in the French Chamber of Deputies . . .', it
gradually changed into a broader, more radical body
of African politicians and trades unionists. The assistant
secretary of the 1945 conference was Jomo Kenyatta:
the joint political secretaries were Kwame Nkrumah
and his friend George Padmore. Padmore, a life-long
admirer of Du Bois and the historian of Panafricanism,[1]
took over much of the initiative of the movement in
Du Bois' old age, and in 1958 joined Nkrumah in
Ghana as his adviser on Panafrican affairs until he died
in September 1959. Like Du Bois, he was not from
Africa: he was born in the West Indies, and spent
most of his life in London, organizing and agitating
for African liberation. He was a Marxist who soon
clashed with the Stalinist régime and their dictatorial
policies for Africa, and he then maintained an almost
equal dislike for Western and Russian domination.
Panafricanism, according to Padmore, 'rejects the un-
bridled system of monopoly capitalism of the West no
less than the political and cultural totalitarianism of the
East'. Padmore was as anti-Communist as only an ex-
Communist can be: though he kept a loyal admiration
for Du Bois, the clash between the two had become
obvious.

The fact that Panafrica was invented by a West
Indian and developed by an American and another
West Indian had not controlled its character. Though
the seeds were sown from abroad, the fruit has become

[1] George Padmore: *Panafricanism or Communism?*, Dennis Dobson,
1956.

essentially African—perhaps too African for some of the sowers : and the emphasis has completely shifted from Negro racialism to African nationalism.

After the war, and the 1945 Congress at Manchester, the impetus towards African unity grew rapidly. In 1949 there was a conference of Asian and African nations at New Delhi, and the next year the 'Afro-Asian' bloc was established within the United Nations, as an expression of the new 'uncommitted' nations led by India. In 1955 came the Bandung Conference in Indonesia, where delegates representing half the world's total population assembled from twenty-five independent nations in Asia and Africa—but predominantly from Arab Africa. They met to consolidate a Third World Force, a force dedicated to peaceful reconciliation of the two great powers.

But at Bandung there was some resentment of Asian domination, and Africa was determined to have its own unity. After the independence of Ghana in March 1957, there were two rival leaders of the African side of the Afro-Asian group—Egypt and Ghana. Kwame Nkrumah immediately announced that he would summon a Panafrican Congress in Ghana : a few weeks later Colonel Nasser sent out invitations to an Afro-Asian People's Solidarity Conference in Cairo, to be held in January 1958. The Cairo conference was not altogether a success. The fact that Russia and China were invited without Britain and America led many Africans to believe that it was too Eastern : while the Russians were disappointed by Nasser's evident caution. The conference decided to set up a permanent body in Cairo, with ten secretaries from

African and Asian states : but less than half of them arrived.

The first real all-African conferences on African soil were in Ghana. The first, in April 1958, was a conference of the independent African states—eight of them, still predominantly Arab : Ghana, Liberia, Morocco, Tunisia, Libya, Egypt, Sudan and Ethiopia. The second, and more important, was the All-African People's Conference in December 1958—a meeting of delegates from sixty-two organizations, representing nationalist movements all over the continent, whether independent or not. It was the sixth, and much the most important, of the Panafrican Congresses held since 1919. It may come to be regarded as the most important African event since the Conference of Berlin seventy-two years before, when the European 'scramble for Africa' was first recognized and legalized. The presence of Nkrumah's Rolls-Royce outside the conference hall symbolized the change in African status that had occurred since the previous conference thirteen years earlier.

The Accra Panafrican conference was in many ways confused and muddled, particularly between French and English speaking delegates. There were a few serious omissions—including Northern Nigeria and the big French African Party, the RDA. Much of the speechmaking consisted of old-fashioned attacks on imperialism. But the conference was a shining symbol for Africans everywhere, for it showed Africans taking the initiative, and tackling the kind of diplomatic decisions which had before always been managed by Europeans.

The dominant theme was, of course, anti-colonialism,

summed up in the banner above the conference hall, saying 'Hands off Africa', and in the words of the Chairman, Tom Mboya, 'Scram out of Africa'. But apart from this negative policy, there were hints of the New Continent.

Africans were determined to avoid commitment to either power bloc: it was the whole point of the conference that they should express their independence, not only as states, but as a continent. It was ironic that Dr. Du Bois, the father of Panafrica, at the age of ninety, should send his wife with a message that was entirely out of tune with this spirit of African uncommitment. Like some other American Negro intellectuals—notably Richard Wright—Du Bois had become disillusioned by the bourgeois character of Independent Africa. 'You cannot choose between Socialism and Private Capitalism, because Private Capitalism is doomed ! . . . the African tribe, whence all of you sprung, was communistic from its very beginnings. . . . There is no trace of private enterprise or individual initiative. . . . You can starve a while longer rather than sell your great heritage for a mess of Western capitalistic potage. . . . Africa awake, put on the beautiful robes of Panafrican Socialism !'

But the 'beautiful robes' caused little enthusiasm, and Du Bois' insistence that Africa should ally herself with the East came only as an embarrassment to the African leaders. The Pygmalion which Du Bois had helped to create had achieved a powerful life of its own. "If the big power blocs have nothing better to do than to fight each other", said Mboya, "let them do so outside Africa: we do not want certain people to take advantage of our social and economic

under-development for their own queer ends: we will not
tolerate *any* country undermining our independence."
"Some of us", said Nkrumah, in opening the conference, "need reminding that Africa is a continent on
its own. It is not an extension of Europe or any other
continent. . . . Do not let us forget that colonialism
and imperialism may come to us yet in a different
guise—not necessarily from Europe."

This and other speeches showed that Africans were
thinking not only of the West in their attacks on imperialism. The mix-up of ideologies at the conference
was well shown in the variety of slogans chosen for
the new Panafrica. Outside the hall there was a banner
proclaiming: 'Long Live the Union of African Republics': but most African speakers preferred to use
the phrases: 'Commonwealth of African Nations' or
'United States of Africa'. Though there was plenty of
idealism there was, in the words of one observer, a
'total absence of any spiritual note'.

The rivalry between Accra and Cairo, or between
Black and Arab Africa, was revealed in the open dis-
agreements between them, particularly on the subject
of Israel, with whom Ghana is very friendly. The
question of whether or not Arab Africa has become
part of the continent as a whole, and if so who will
lead it, will become an increasingly important one.
The old division of 'Africa South of the Sahara' may
well, at a time when the Sahara itself is ceasing to be
a barrier, prove out-of-date. The play of Arab politics
on the rest of Africa can certainly not be ignored: but
it seems likely that as more African states become independent, so they will resent any attempt at Cairo
leadership.

On one crucial point the Arabs and Africans had come into sharp argument—on the question of violence. Delegates from South of the Sahara wished to include non-violence as a basic principle in the resolutions, but the Algerian delegation threatened to walk out unless the conference supported their own use of violence. The quarrel was settled with a compromise declaration which, although clearly the result of Algerian pressure, was later held by Europeans in Africa —particularly in Central Africa—to contribute a general sanction for violence everywhere :

"Recognizing that national independence can be gained by peaceful means in territories where democratic means are available, the conference guarantees its support to all forms of peaceful action. This support is pledged equally to those who, in order to meet the violent means by which they are subjected and exploited, are obliged to retaliate."

The conference ended with a series of bold resolutions, including the promise to boycott South African goods, to set up a 'Freedom Fund' to help nationalist movements, and to form a permanent Panafrican secretariat in Accra, to co-ordinate the new nations of Africa.

So Panafrica came into being, in name if not in fact. The ideal of many of the leaders has been that it should lead ultimately to a re-drawing of the old artificial frontiers, to African federations and closer unions, similar to that celebrated just before the conference, between Ghana and former French Guinea. In what has been called 'the new scramble for Africa', Ghana is not the only state which will be looking to see how it can extend its influence and economy. The dazzling picture of the United States, with a huge common market and common interest, is the goal of many Panafricanists. How far can this succeed, between vigorous African leaders who have dedicated their lives to national independence? Or will Africa be split and 'balkanized' into small, proud, touchy and insecure states at loggerheads with one another?

The long-term outcome of Panafrica has yet to be seen. But the immediate results of the Accra conference were soon magnified. The European Press, having largely ignored the conference at the time, soon blamed it for a whole series of upheavals—in the Congo, Kenya, Nyasaland or Rhodesia. Among Whites, Accra very quickly ceased to be a joke and became a bogey, almost equal to Moscow—if not part of Moscow—in its alleged power over Africa. But while the West saw the hand of Russia at Accra, the Russian observer, Professor Potekhin, saw the heavy hand of America.

No evidence has been produced of a direct connection between Accra and the Congo or Nyasaland riots, and many of the allegations against Accra seem only a new form of the old desire to provide an external scapegoat for internal troubles. But indirectly, there can be no doubt that the Panafrican congresses have quickened the pace of African discontent. It was probably the main achievement of the December meeting that it provided a synchronization of African movements—setting the African leaders alongside each other, reprimanding the laggards and beckoning them to the front. At the same time Accra did provide a kind of African headquarters, however temporary, which acted as a mouthpiece for 'African opinion', to encourage the militants and prod the moderates.

PART TWO

CHAPTER I

"GHANA!"

FOR THE PAST seven years, there has been only one independent African state which has attracted the notice of the world. Of the other two, Ethiopia is Hamitic, not Negro, and usually considered outside 'Black Africa': and Liberia is largely dominated by America. When people have talked about Black Africa, they have meant Ghana. The small slice of tropical country, tucked under the paunch of Africa with four and a half million people, has become the sole symbol of black independence—the crucial experiment to show whether Africans can rule themselves. In the White-dominated countries, 'Ghana!' is a cry of confidence and hope in the black townships, and pictures of Dr. Nkrumah hang in the cubby-holes of voteless black office-boys. Among the Whites, Ghana has been the favourite argument against yielding to African nationalism.

This lonely eminence has been an advantage and a snag. It has given Ghana a long lead over the other African nations to establish herself as the 'lodestar' of Africa: in international diplomacy, Nkrumah has gained a fame far greater than that of Asian leaders of ten times his power. But the uniqueness, too, has placed Ghana in the full glare of curiosity, aggravated by every kind of bias. Advocates of white supremacy have waited to gloat over black administration, while negrophiles have been easily disillusioned by the discovery that Africans can make their own mistakes.

Ghana is not typical of Africa, and it is largely a quirk of history that has pushed it ahead of other states. It is more volatile and more educated than most African territories, and the richest area in tropical Africa, with an annual income per head of £55 (1955). Though there have been trading settlements and European forts—first Portuguese, then Dutch, then Danish, then English—since the sixteenth century, their hold was not strong, and in the eighteenth century a governor was flogged and imprisoned. It is only since 1850 that the southern part of Ghana has been a British colony. The combination of an agricultural middle class and a small white settlement—only five thousand at the time of independence—encouraged Britain to institute limited African elections as early as 1925, long before most other African states.

The equatorial coast to which Ghana belongs stands to the rest of Africa somewhat as the Mediterranean to Europe, or the coast of South-East Asia to the rest of Asia. In spite of the appalling traffic in slaves, estimated at twenty million until the abolition in 1807, it is an area without racial feelings against Europeans. It is hot, lazy, easy-going and able—except for the arid Northern Territories—to live happily off the land. The West Coast has a frothy, extrovert character, mercurial and emotional, in which passions quickly rise and fall, like Italy's. Politics, though fierce, sound often fiercer than they are, and the frontiers of laughter are baffling. In its woolliness, West Africa is more like

Ceylon than Central or East Africa, and more tropical than African.

Accra, the sea-port capital of Ghana, is one of the most exotic cities in the continent. No doubt its strangeness and charm, and its total contrast with Europe, has helped its reputation as typical of Africa—whose cities can often be as depressing as Europe's. In Accra tall men in brightly-coloured togas and sandals walk through the noisy markets, with a blaze of Elizabethan extroversion—including Elizabethan open sewers—and Roman grandeur. Huge carved canoes with bare-backed oarsmen carry crates from the ships at anchor. There are palm-wine bars, an eating-place called 'Café de Mr. You,' a night-club called 'Kalamazoo Shake Your Head' and rickety lorries with hand-painted mottoes which sum up the grandiose optimism of Ghana: 'Here Comes Black Eagle', 'Big Boy No. 4'.

In the middle of Accra stands the modern airy building, with a mace, a copy of Erskine May, and a black speaker with a white wig, which has come to be regarded as the outward symbol of African Democracy. In its division between Government and Opposition benches, its parliamentary procedure and representatives elected by universal suffrage, it is a close copy of Westminster.

The development of democratic Ghana has been quick and abrupt. Its history hangs on one momentous day in 1948. Early in that year, the post-war troubles of Ghana—then the Gold Coast—had come to a head. Ex-servicemen had come back to their country to find limited opportunities, and growing unemployment. The cost of living was rising sharply, and the cocoa trees—the crucial crop on which Ghana's wealth depended—were dying of 'swollen shoot'—which could only be stopped by drastic Government orders to cut down trees.

Into this discontented country came the gay, calculating figure of Kwame Nkrumah, hailed by his followers as 'Showboy'. He returned to the Gold Coast as a bachelor of thirty-eight in 1947, after studying at Lincoln, Pennsylvania and (very briefly) at the London School of Economics, where he had picked up a Marxist training, a Western sense of organization, and an over-riding ambition to liberate his country. He combined two complementary characters: he had dazzling showmanship and simple demagoguery, together with a shrewd understanding of political organization: he was able to be African in a European way. Nkrumah shook the wobbly tree of the Gold Coast, and the fruits fell all around him.

The ex-servicemen's anger culminated on February 28—a day celebrated by an avenue in Accra—with a march to the Governor's Castle to demand an interview: the procession was halted by police and in the following skirmish two Africans were shot dead. They were the only two martyrs of the Gold Coast Revolution, but they were sufficient to set off the public anger: in the next two days European shops were burnt and looted and, although the police deliberately kept away, twenty-nine people were killed.

February 28 set off a quick chain of events. Nkrumah, and the others of the 'Big Six' of the African leaders, were detained for two months under emergency powers. In the meantime the Labour government in London appointed a commission of enquiry

under a British K.C., Aiken Watson, which criticized
the administration and recommended greater African
participation. Soon afterwards, Britain took the revolutionary step of appointing an all-African committee
under an African judge, Sir Henley Coussey, to pro-
pose constitutional changes. They proposed giving
Ghana a British form of government, with universal
suffrage and an African cabinet, with only three white
ministers and reserved powers for the Governor. With
modifications, the Colonial Office accepted it : Ghana
was set unmistakably on the road to independence.

Returning from exile, Nkrumah seized his chance
for leadership : he broke away from the United Gold
Coast Convention, the middle-class party which
had first invited him back to the country, to form his
own 'Convention People's Party', demanding 'Self-
government *Now*!', and 'Free*dom*'. With modern
methods, nationalistic slogans and mass meetings he
quickly outbid the more cautious bourgeois leaders,
who were to become his greatest enemies. To rally his
party, Nkrumah organized a campaign of 'positive
action', which culminated in a general strike. Nkrumah and others were arrested, tried and convicted for
organizing an illegal strike, and sentenced to two
years' imprisonment.

While Nkrumah was in jail, the first general elections under the new constitution were organized :
Nkrumah's party won thirty-four out of thirty-eight
constituencies, and there followed one of the most
dramatic half-hours in colonial history. A deputation
from the CPP called on the new Governor, Sir Charles
Arden Clarke, at his Castle to demand their leader's
release, to be told : 'Gentlemen, if you go out in the

streets you will find he is already at large.' The same
day, the Governor met Nkrumah for the first time,
and offered him the post of Leader of Government
Business, to be virtual Prime Minister of the Gold
Coast.

For the next six years, the Government rested on
the strange alliance of Prime Minister and Governor,
who represented the new system and the old. Arden-
Clarke was a tough, red-faced proconsul with a con-
ventional colonial career behind him. But he was also
a realist: he found that he could trust his African colleagues, who trusted him. On March 6, 1957—the
anniversary of the Bond of 1844, the 'Magna Carta'
signed between the Chiefs and the British Government—the Gold Coast became the independent state
of Ghana.

Self-government quickly brought its troubles: for
two years beforehand there had been a menacing op-
position to Nkrumah, which had caused the date of
independence to be postponed. The opposition was led
by the intellectuals and professional men whose power
Nkrumah had neatly by-passed—who formed first the
'National Liberation Movement', and then the 'United
Party' under the leadership of a quiet but indignant
Professor of Sociology educated at Cambridge, Dr.
Busia. He was uneasily allied with the tribal Chiefs
and their followers, centring on the old kingdom of
Ashanti in the middle of Ghana, who were hostile to
the upstart revolutionaries from Accra. The Chiefs
and professional leaders had always regarded themselves as heirs-apparent to British rule: the rift between Nkrumah and the Chiefs was partly a projection
of the rift between two different phases of British

colonial policy—between 'indirect rule' through Chiefs, and full democracy.

Nkrumah believed that there could be no compromise between the Chiefs and modern democracy. he was determined to 'take the Chief out of politics'. His fight against the Chieftancy was in some ways similar to the fight of the Commons against the monarchy in eighteenth-century England, but telescoped into a few years. The speed and ruthlessness with which Nkrumah had to act, transferring the power of Chiefs in local councils to his party nominees, left a raw anger in the old centres of privilege.

Frustrated and disunited, and with no tradition of parliamentary protest, the opposition resorted to threats of violence and secession, and agitation by tribal groups. The disappearance of the British bogy had removed the major spur to unity, and Ghana was in obvious danger of 'fissiparous tendencies'.

Six months after independence day, Nkrumah returned to Ghana from a Commonwealth conference to find signs of tribal agitation, a divided Cabinet, indignation about the low cocoa prices, his car booed in the streets and some outspoken criticism of his high-handedness. Nkrumah was determined to 'show who is governing the country'. A newspaper columnist from Sierra Leone, Bankole Timothy, who wrote an article called 'What Next, Kwame?' was promptly deported without trial, followed soon after by other foreign-born opposition supporters. A new Minister of the Interior was appointed—later moved to Communications—who seemed to sum up the wilder side of the New Ghana. Krobo Edusei was a short, tough demagogue from Ashanti, who had been condemned in a

1954 report on corruption as 'unfit for public office'. He understood the African mind much better than he understood the West. Known as the 'Minister of Noise', or 'The Angel of Death', he had an uncanny knack of crowd-pleasing, with a mixture of loud humour and serious threats, and a closeness to the urban masses which Nkrumah now lacked.

A year later, at the end of 1958, came further crises: an opposition plot called 'Zenith Seven' was allegedly uncovered. Strong new bills were passed, among them an act to control trades unions and a Preventive Detention Bill—based on a British colonial act, passed but never used, allowing detention for five years without trial. Two months later, two of the leading opposition M.P.s were detained under the new Bill for having allegedly planned a *coup* involving Army NCO's.

Living in the Governor's Castle, moving through Accra in a Rolls-Royce with an escort of motor-cycles, and hardly venturing at that time to the stormy areas of Ashanti, Nkrumah soon looked very different from the 'Showboy' of his revolutionary days. The opposition intellectuals taunted him with references to George Orwell's *Animal Farm*, the story of pigs who led a successful revolt against their farmer, only to take on the same characteristics as the hated human. 'Napoleon the Pig' became their favourite nickname for Nkrumah.

Many of Nkrumah's strong-arm actions could be justified in what he called the 'rough-and-tumble' of Ghana politics. He had never suggested that black government would be easy: the slogan of his paper had been 'Self-government with danger is better than servitude in tranquillity', and in his 'Motion of Destiny' demanding independence in July 1953 he had said : 'As long as we are ruled by others we shall lay our mistakes at their door and our sense of responsibility will remain dulled.'

There were many valid reasons why Nkrumah was pressed to deviate from British methods of democracy : the very existence of the State, as opposed to rival tribes, was something hardly realized. In a country obsessed with political feuds, the separation between politics, civil service and judiciary was still only partial. The exodus of many British civil servants had left few Africans trained for higher posts : the few British who remained were criticized by fellow-Europeans for condoning Nkrumah's actions. The gaps in government and the inefficiency of the police made it difficult for Nkrumah to suppress the opposition plots, some of which were genuine enough, without drastic and un-British methods.

There was no bill which Nkrumah passed, as he hastened to point out, which had not its parallel in white-ruled Africa. The same phrases about 'small bands of agitators', 'foreign infiltrations', 'public safety' were used in Kenya and Rhodesia, and in the colonial Gold Coast. Deportations and detentions have been common in British colonies—the only difference being the (often formal) declarations of emergencies. But the idealism and hope on which Ghana had been founded, with the slogan 'Freedom and Justice', quickly faded in the face of its practical problems, and the radiant example of Ghana among Africans elsewhere lost some of its first lustre.

No doubt an 'African way of doing things', as Nkrumah has called it, will gradually change the shape of Ghana, and the democratic formalities of the British

House of Commons seem very irrelevant in the hot
and angry air of Accra. "It is necessary in Ghana", said
Nkrumah soon after independence, "to impose by a
positive discipline what in the older democracies is
done subconciously." The idea that African democracy
should follow the pattern of Westminster, with its own
unusual history, was never very confidently held.
Britain bequeathed to Ghana a black House of Commons, not in the belief that it was ideally suited to
Africa, but because it was the only form of Government she knew.

There is much that is alarming and unattractive to
Europeans in the new face of Ghana: the growing
bribery, the immense powers of Nkrumah's party, and
the 'personality cult' of the leader, with his head on
coins and stamps, and a statue outside the assembly.
But the politics of Ghana are never as harsh and dangerous as they sound; the mixture of threats, rumours,
bombast and laughter is never easy to disentangle. In
spite of the domination of the Convention People's
Party, Ghana is not yet a dictatorship which can afford
to disregard the popular vote. Much of the legacy of
British rule, it is true, has already disappeared, including the independence of the police, judiciary, and civil
service. The democracy of Ghana is unlikely to be a
disciplined two-party parliament on the British pattern. But once the foundations of the state have been
laid, it may possibly devise an 'African way of doing
things' which offers safety without tyranny.

But the future of Ghana will be closely linked with
the future of West Africa. By 1960 she will no longer
be blazing a lonely African trail; she will be a small,
unusual neighbour to the far more powerful state of

Nigeria. Ghana may suffer from losing her pre-eminence and fame: but she will also lose much of the awkward tension and uncertainty of her perch. For underneath many of Ghana's troubles lies a lingering lack of confidence, from generations of slave-raids and subjugation, and a lurking doubt as to whether Africans really *can* rule themselves.

CHAPTER II

WEST AFRICAN JIGSAW

GHANA IS ONLY a small part of the huge bulge
known as West Africa, bordered on the west and
south by the sea, on the north by the Sahara and
Algeria, and on the east by the long, desolate strip
of French Equatorial Africa. The coast of West Africa
was discovered by the Portuguese in the late fifteenth
century, and isolated European forts and trading posts
were soon established, dealing in ivory, gold, slaves or
palm-oil. It was not till the nineteenth century, with
travellers like Mungo Park, who discovered the Niger,
that the interior was mapped and frontiers established.

West Africa now consists of one mass of French
West Africa, out of which bites of territory have been
taken all along the southern coast by Britain, Portugal
and Liberia. Thus the coastal countries—the richest
and most important part of West Africa—are alter-
nately French and non-French—reading from west
to east : Senegal, Gambia, Senegal, Portuguese Guinea,
French Guinea, Sierra Leone, Liberia, Ivory Coast,
Ghana, the trust territories of Togoland, Dahomey,
Nigeria. Above these coastal regions are the vast and
dry French African provinces of Mauritania, French
Sudan, the Upper Volta and Niger, stretching into the
Sahara Desert.

Nowhere is the chaos of the 'scramble for Africa'
more apparent than in this complicated jigsaw of territories : the confusion has been further irritated by the

lack of contact between the French and English colonies, which have had almost directly opposite systems of colonial rule. Few people have a close knowledge of both sides of West Africa : when Englishmen refer to West Africa they nearly always mean 'British West Africa', ignoring three-quarters of the area. In fact, the development of French Africa may well be the more important.

Until two years ago, French Africa had scarcely an impact on the rest of the continent. It was insulated partly by the barrier of language, but mainly by the close ties between the French African leaders and Paris. To pass from British to French Africa is like leaving Africa for France—black architecture, cafés, society or manners seem all more French than African. It has been a cardinal principle in French policy that her colonies should be regarded as part of the metropolitan country : and this has been partially achieved—up till 1959—by giving Africans seats in the Chamber of Deputies, and by the development of the *évolués*, the small élite of educated Africans who have been absorbed into European life. The *évolués* are far more French than British Africans are British : Paris has been their capital, and the French parliament their centre of gravity.

The most important African figure in post-war French Africa has been the urbane and metropolitan Deputy from the Ivory Coast, Felix Houphouet-Boigny, who founded the massive French African party, the *Rassemblement Democratique Africain*, in 1946. He presents an utter contrast with Nkrumah, which could be said to represent the contrast between the two colonial systems. Houphouet is the wealthy son of a chief, with a tribal background and a middle-class milieu: as such he would have been doomed in Ghana. But in French West Africa he has succeeded in combining a strong hold on his people, based on earlier organization of strikes and boycotts, with an important role in Paris politics. He began by collaborating with the Communists, when they were part of the post-war French government; but broke with them when their disruptive aims had become clear, to ally his party, the RDA, with a French left-wing group, the UDSR. Since then he has become almost the Vicar of Bray of French politics, serving as Minister in five successive governments, including de Gaulle's Fifth Republic.

The French system has meant that, while Ghana and Nigeria were moving to independence, French Africa was still bound to France, without autonomy. An immense change came in 1956, hardly noticed in Britain, when a comprehensive *loi-cadre* or 'outline-law' was drafted under Mollet's Socialist Government, with the help of Houphouet. Prompted by the disasters of Indo-China, the bitter war in Algeria and the looming independence of British Africa, the French Government agreed to major steps towards African democracy, including African cabinets in each of the eight provinces of French West Africa, elected by universal suffrage. But the new law stopped short of granting independence: the African prime ministers worked alongside a Governor responsible to Paris. The catchword of the new constitution was 'interdependence' rather than 'independence'. Though it represented a huge stride forward for African autonomy, overtaking most of British West Africa in one bold law, it was also a step towards a dangerous new condition—the 'balkanization' of West Africa—by giving separate territories their own self-government.

The Paris compromise gave French African politics a more sophisticated character than the strident nationalism of the British states next door. The *évolué* leaders were as much concerned with French politics as with African politics, and they saw the strong economic benefits of the tie with France : they were concerned more with the realities of their status than with the outward show of independence.

But it was also clear that African national ambitions could not be restrained for long. De Gaulle, coming into power in May 1958, realized that his only chance of maintaining a connection with black Africa, after the disasters of Algeria, lay in a much looser alliance. Though Africans were at first suspicious of this liberalism, it seemed increasingly apparent that de Gaulle wished to be regarded as the Liberator of Africa. He embarked on a dramatic tour of Africa, accompanied by Houphouet, then one of his four senior ministers. They offered all the French African territories—eight in West Africa, four in Equatorial Africa—the simple choice between complete independence and becoming part of the new Afro-French 'Community', which replaced the ineffectual old 'French Union'. They were to have a large share of self-government, but with matters such as defence, foreign policy or currency regulated by the Federal Community.

In every country, encouraged by the leaders, de Gaulle's offer was well received, except in French Guinea ; there he encountered the uncompromising thirty-six-year-old Prime Minister, Sekou Touré, who, in the course of a speech in de Gaulle's presence, said, "Guinea prefers poverty in freedom to riches in slavery." De Gaulle, taking it as an insult to France, lost his temper: "Then all you have to do is to vote 'No'," he replied. "I promise nobody will stand in the way of your independence." The following month the referendum took place; French Guinea, alone of all the French territories, voted 'No' to the new constitution, and on September 29, 1958, became the first independent state from French Africa. Thus Guinea, having been primarily part of France, became suddenly part of Africa.

The secession of Guinea precipitated a division in the biggest French African party, the RDA, and brought to a climax the old rivalry between two leaders —Sekou Touré and Houphouet-Boigny, Prime Minister of the next-door Ivory Coast. Touré was much closer to the type of British African nationalist, and particularly to Nkrumah: like him, he had a Marxist training, a gift of gay oratory, and a strong opposition to the Chiefs and middle-class leaders. Touré, twenty years younger than Houphouet, had never been absorbed into Paris politics: he was largely self-educated, rebellious from the beginning, and proud of his grandfather, a heroic Guinea Chief who had fought the French to the last.

The first French state to appear on the African stage was much poorer than Ghana, dependent on France for a subsidy of seven million pounds a year. Because of this, and the lingering cultural affinity, independent Guinea still looked to Paris for alliance and assistance. But de Gaulle—though he partly relented—was unwilling to assist the odd one out: instead, Sekou Touré, in a spectacular *coup*, reached a sudden agreement with Nkrumah, his next-but-one neighbour along the coast, for a union between the two countries, with a loan of ten million pounds from Ghana to Guinea.

The Ghana-Guinea union was much looser than it sounded, and made still vaguer by the fact that Nkrumah knew no French, and Sekou Touré no English. The practical difficulties of a union between two countries separated by four hundred miles of unsympathetic Ivory Coast, with no common language, tribe or culture, were unique. But though the alliance was mocked by larger neighbours, it was a challenge. For the past forty years, ever since a West African National Congress was formed in London in 1920, a Federation of West African States had been the dream of black leaders. There was a mounting danger that, with the retreat of the French and British Empires, West Africa would be 'balkanized' into small and scarcely viable rival states. The creation of Ghana-Guinea was undeniably the first step towards the creation of the United States of Africa.

With the emergence of independent Ghana and Guinea, and greater self-rule in French African territories, the fitting together of the jigsaw pieces in West Africa became suddenly more urgent. The frozen block of French West Africa had begun to thaw at the edges, and new conglomerations were quickly planned. In April 1959, two territories of French West Africa—Senegal and Soudan—combined under the presidency of Leopold Senghor to form the 'Mali Federation' within the French Community, named after a thirteenth-century African empire, and with the slogan : 'one people, one aim, one faith.'

In the next ten years, the whole map of West Africa is likely to change: it has become part of Africa's diplomacy, not Europe's. A 'United States of West Africa' is the goal of many African states: but the rivalries and diversities, with different colonial up-bringings superimposed on their different tribes, present alarming obstacles. However pressing the reasons for union, the antipathies are sharp.

Most difficult are the two coastal states in the middle of West Africa, Sierra Leone and Liberia, which have been described as 'black settler' colonies. Both of them were founded by freed slaves, who were shipped back to Africa in a spirit of idealism. Sierra Leone was colonized by Negro settlers from England as early as 1787, later joined by thousands of slaves rescued from ships by the British Navy: their settle-ment—now the capital of the colony—was proudly called Freetown. But while the colonists were relatively free, the native Africans were not: and the Creoles, as the mixed descendants of the first immigrants were called, remained a black aristocracy, dominating and scorning the native majority. With the beginnings of African democracy in Sierra Leone since the war, the Creoles lost much of their political power: but the cross-purposes between the fifty thousand Creoles and the two million Africans remains a stumbling-block in the way of independence.

More embarrassing is the next-door country, Liberia, which was founded thirty-four years after Sierra Leone by a first batch of twenty-one freed American Negroes, and likewise named as the 'Land of the Free'—with the blessing and protection of America. Here, too, the descendants of the settlers became a master-race—and

in this case have remained so. Though elections are
held, there is usually only one candidate, from the
'True Whig Party'—the party of the Americo-
Liberians, as the descendants of the pioneers call
themselves. Though they number only about 15,000
out of one and a half million, their hold on the country
is kept by tight economic control, helped by the il-
literacy of the indigenous people. For a century
Liberia was the only independent black nation (apart
from Ethiopia), but it has been so poor, so corrupt and
so financially dominated by America—notably the
Firestone Rubber Corporation—that it has been more
of an embarrassment than a source of pride. To the
emerging independent states along the West Coast,
Liberia is not encouraging: though Nkrumah and
William Tubman, the wily President of Liberia,
have struck up a formal diplomatic friendship,
Tubman is naturally wary of the mass democracy
both of Ghana and of Guinea, on his northern
frontier. He would hardly welcome a West African
Federation.

Two other odd segments are Gambia and Portuguese Guinea, at the west end of West Africa. The
Gambia is the smallest and absurdest English colony,
with three hundred thousand Africans on a thin strip
of territory on either side of the Gambia River, jutting
into the middle of the French territory of Senegal.
A union of Gambia with Senegal, of which it forms a
natural part, would give Gambia more trade, and
Senegal its natural waterway: but the Chiefs of Gambia, who still maintain much of their power, are
alarmed by the universal suffrage in Senegal, and remain loyally pro-British. Portuguese Guinea remains

so far insulated against democracy in French Guinea to the west or Senegal to the north.

A key piece in the West African puzzle is the wealthy territory of the Ivory Coast, with only two million people, but nearly as rich as Ghana, with a large new artificial harbour at Abidjan and considerable exports of diamonds, bananas and cocoa. The wealth of the Ivory Coast underpins the power of the Premier, Houphouet-Boigny. In 1959 its influence was extended by economic agreements with Upper Volta and Niger to the North: but Houphouet naturally prefers a close relationship with France to friendships with Touré to the West, or Nkrumah to the East. Much depends on whether Houphouet can keep up his balancing-trick between France and Africa.

*   *   *

With all these frictions and divisions, a United States of West Africa is still distant, and there is a serious risk of West Africa splitting up to provide fifteen separate rival states, each a member of the United Nations. But the future of them all will be affected by the one giant country which rests on the 'hinge of Africa', Nigeria.

Nigeria, with thirty-five million people, eight times the population of Ghana and three times that of South Africa, is the most populous territory in Africa, and thirteenth in the world. When it becomes independent on October 1, 1960, the whole balance of power of the continent will be altered: it may become as much a black stronghold as South Africa is for Whites, or Egypt for the Arabs; the Ghana-Guinea Union, or the feuds of French West Africa, could be eclipsed by this large black mass. Nigerians look down on Ghana as a boastful bubble, soon to be pricked by them.

Yet, compared to Ghana, little is known about Nigeria in the world outside. This is partly due to Nigeria's relative poverty (£21 a year per head, compared to Ghana's £55 or the Congo's £25); to its wild hinterland, and to its comparative lack of educated men (about 23,000 children at secondary school, compared with Ghana's 9,000). But more than anything, the world's haziness about Nigeria is due to the doubt as to its existence as a state at all. It was invented by Lord Lugard in 1914, when the two protectorates of Southern and Northern Nigeria were amalgamated into a single colony. Before 1900 the Northern part was a vague administration by the Royal Niger Company—later to become Unilever—which traded in ground-nuts along the river Niger: while the South consisted of two narrow coastal protectorates. The tribes, the histories and traditions of the different corners of Nigeria have no connection except British domination; of all the odd creations of colonial Africa, the square shape of Nigeria is the oddest.

For this reason, there has always been debate as to whether Nigeria could become a single independent state. Since 1914 it has been administered as three separate regions, East, West and North—the last having its own system of Moslem laws and government. Only since 1946 has Nigeria had a central parliament, at the coastal capital of Lagos—itself a bone of regional contention.

The three regions are as different as they could be, and each is headed by a strong and typical Prime Minister. The biggest, with nearly half the population,

is the North, which is predominantly Moslem and
in some ways closer in character to North Africa
than the West Coast. It is feudal, poor and undeveloped, and still dominated by Chieftains, or Emirs.
Most of the people are a Negroid group of tribes, the
Hausas: but in the early nineteenth century, the
Hausas were conquered by a light-skinned Hamitic
people, the Fulani, who still form most of the ruling
class, though intermarried with their vassals. The
Prime Minister of the Northern Region, himself a
descendant of the Fulani Kings, is the Sardauna (a
nephew of the Sultan) of Sokoto, the Moslem holy
city of the North. He is a handsome, courteous aristo-
crat who has come to terms only partly with modern
democracy. He combines feudal authority with the
leadership of the mass Northern People's Congress;
but he has previously urged the delaying of Nigerian
independence, because he felt that Southern administrators would swamp his country. Like the Ashanti
in Ghana, or the Southerners in Sudan, the Fulani
have regarded the British more as protectors than
oppressors.

The Eastern Region—east of the Niger, which bi-
sects the South—is mainly inhabited by the Ibos, the
most lively and go-ahead people in West Africa. They
are one of the many peoples (Kikuyu, Xhosa, Nyasas)
who have been called 'The Jews of Africa': and because the Eastern Region is poor and overcrowded,
they have overflowed into the other two regions, where
they run much of the business and civil service. Their
Premier is one of the most colourful Africans in the
continent, Dr. Nnamdi Azikiwe, better known as Zik.
Like Nkrumah, who is five years his junior, and still

his friend, he was educated at the American Howard University : he entered Nigerian politics with American thoroughness, creating a powerful political machine and founding several concerns, including a bank and a chain of virulent newspapers. One of the earliest African nationalists, he seemed at one time likely to dominate the whole of Nigeria with his party, the 'National Council of Nigeria and the Cameroons', and his demagogy called 'Zikism'. His political bark was much worse than his bite : he has deftly combined wild anti-British speeches with a private insistence that Britain should keep close ties with his country.

Zik's principal rival is the Prime Minister of the Western Region, Chief Obafemi Awolowo, who is the dead opposite of Zik and Nkrumah. He is an ambitious, ascetic intellectual of fifty, an orphan who worked his way from grim poverty to become a barrister in London. He founded his party, the Action Group, to oust Zik's party from Western Nigeria—in which he largely succeeded—and to demand independence for his people, the Yorubas. The three million Yorubas in Western Nigeria—a third of the population—are the proud descendants from the ancient Yoruba Kingdoms which dominated West Africa up to the sixteenth century : they resent both the infiltration of the Ibos and the conservatism of the Hausas.

But both Yorubas and Ibos are lively and ambitious people : the South of Nigeria stands to Ghana in some ways as America stands to Britain. It is ambitious, capitalistic, ruthless, and bent on obtaining the maximum of foreign capital. The tours of the Nigerian leaders—particularly Awolowo—to the Western countries to stimulate investment, have become legendary for their lavishness and public relations—typified by the unprecedented appearance in 1958 of a full-page advertisement for Western Nigeria in *The Times*.

The regions of Nigeria remain an uneasy trio. The titular Prime Minister of the Federal Parliament is a modern young Northern Moslem, Abubakar Tafawa Balewa, who has so far succeeded partially in combining the following of the Northern People's Party with leadership over the South. But the power of Nigeria remains largely in the regional Parliament: and each region has its minorities, terrified of the consequences of independence. With their country only forty-five years old, the people still think of themselves less as Nigerians than as Yorubas or Ibos. For the past eight years, the obstacle to independence has been not Britain but themselves. When a constitutional conference was held in London in 1953, to plan the path to self-determination, the unity of the regions seemed unlikely, except under the loosest of Federations. But in the following five years the attractions of a single state, and the obvious dangers of three small ones, became stronger: so that when the second constitutional conference was held in London in 1958, the mood was very different. With elaborate safeguards for minorities, a strong central government was agreed by all three regions. Nigerians now hope that the three regional parties, instead of trisecting the state, will provide the safeguards and political competition which Ghana lacks. The troubles of Ghana, with its own division between the Coast, Ashanti and the North, have been taken to heart in Nigeria.

Nigeria is still too preoccupied with herself to think much about West African federation: but if she does remain together, much of the rest of West Africa may unite with or against her. The existence of a prosperous Nigeria will be a challenge to the whole of French West Africa. The 'new scramble for Africa', a contest not by Europeans but Africans, may ironically be a scramble between French- and English-speaking Africa.

CHAPTER III

CONGO DREAM

To the west of Nigeria lie two strips of trust territory, the (small) British and (large) French Cameroons—both deriving, like other African trusteeships, from a German colony before the First World War. Both will emerge to independence in 1960 with the exception of the Northern half of the British trusteeship, which has become part of Northern Nigeria. Both seem likely to request reunification, forming a single new state of four million people alongside Nigeria.

Beyond the Cameroons is the central mass of the continent—French Equatorial Africa and the Belgian Congo. They are the dark heart of Africa, where political ideas, conflicts and even frontiers peter out in the heat and poverty. They lie between Libya in the north, and Rhodesia in the south : or between the independent black states to the west and the multi-racial states in the east.

French Equatorial Africa is much poorer and bleaker than French West Africa, which it adjoins on its North-West frontier. It has only a short strip of coastline, between the Cameroons and the Belgian Congo, with one port, Point Noire : the only railway line in the whole of FEA, which is four times the size of France, is the three hundred miles from Point Noire to the capital, Brazzaville—a line which was only completed, under appalling difficulties, in 1934. Once known as the French Congo, FEA consists of four territories, which were grouped together in their present form in 1910—Gabon, Ubangi-Shari, now grandly renamed the Central African Republic, Chad and Middle Congo, now renamed the Congo Republic. Like French West Africa, they were given a greater measure of autonomy in the 1956 outline-law, and again in the De Gaulle constitution of 1958.

The Congo Republic—not to be confused with the Belgian Congo across the river—contains the railway-line, the capital, part of the Congo river and some of the liveliest people. The Prime Minister is a suspended Catholic priest, the Abbé Youlou Fulbert, a short, mild-looking leader who was condemned by the Church in 1956 when he first stood for election. Since then, he has had a spectacular success, deriving prestige both from his status as a priest, and from Rome's condemnation of him. But Fulbert's main appeal lies in his dream to re-unify, not only the four provinces of FEA in a 'United States of Central Africa', but also the legendary empire of the Bacongo.

The Bacongo—after whom the river was named—are one of the proudest tribes of Africa, the descendants of the great Kingdom of the Congo which the Portuguese discovered in 1482, when they landed at the mouth of the river. It was a rich and powerful state, stretching for several hundred miles into the interior, producing ivory, copper, and silver, and sending their own Ambassador to Portugal. The Bacongo, who were subjected and sold in slavery, are now scattered through several African territories—French Congo, Belgian Congo, Portuguese West Africa and the small Portuguese enclave of Cabinda, at the mouth of the river. But they have kept their sense of unity and pride in their cultural traditions, and a leaning towards messianic and spiritual leaders, of whom the Abbé is the latest.

Across the Congo river from Brazzaville, with a hundred thousand inhabitants, is Leopoldville, the capital of the Belgian Congo. The contrast between the two capitals, separated by two and a half miles of fast and muddy river which can be crossed only by ferry, could hardly be more striking. Brazzaville is the capital of one of the poorest regions of Africa : Leopold-ville the capital of the second richest—second only to South Africa.

'Leo', as the Belgian capital is known, is one of the most spectacular cities in Africa, and unlike any other. It has a quarter of a million inhabitants, including only fifteen thousand Whites : but the centre of the town looks as much a white man's city as Johannesburg. The white City consists of a narrow strip along the Congo, with magnificent mansions looking over the river, and a broad boulevard of shops, pavement cafés and office buildings. The black city, consisting of well-organized locations, surrounds the White strip—a situation which makes Leo perilous for Whites in time of trouble.

The Belgian Congo, from which Leo draws its wealth, is almost as large as FEA, and seventy-seven times the size of Belgium, with one and a half times its population (twelve million). Its early history is the most disreputable in Africa : the Congo River, which runs across the North of it, was first explored by Henry Stanley, in 1874, after he had discovered Livingstone. Stanley was then employed by King Leopold of Belgium to sign up the 'Congo Free State', as it was

ironically called, as his own personal property. Until
1909 King Leopold ruled the Congo through an army
of ruthless agents, who made for him a vast personal
fortune from rubber and ivory, by terrorizing the African inhabitants. There were several contemporary ac-
counts of King Leopold's régime : an American Baptist
missionary described how native levies were used to
shoot down rebellious forced labourers : "The hands
—the hands of men, women and children—were
placed in rows before the Commissionaire, who counted
them to see that the natives had not wasted cartridges."
A Swedish missionary, Sjoblom, described how forty-
five towns were burnt down when natives refused to
gather india-rubber.

The British Government sent a consul from Nigeria,
Roger Casement, who wrote a long and damning report. In 1908 the scandal had become so great that
the Congo was annexed by the Belgian Government,
and the reign of terror ended : the Chiefs had been
killed or terrorized, the population reduced (according
to one investigator, E. D. Morel) by one and a half
million, and the whole country demoralized.

The new Belgian system was planned to atone for
the international infamy of King Leopold : and it is
this system under which the Congo is now run. It is
sometimes described as the 'Welfare State' of Africa :
its housing, primary schools, and social amenities are
legendary. But the political amenities have so far been
confined to municipal votes for African mayors and
councils. The Congo is the most striking example of
the theory of 'houses, not votes' : and as such has been
an important study for Whites elsewhere. The belief
behind the Congo system is that, given economic

advancement and decent treatment—together with 'guided' education—Africans will not demand self-rule. Africans can become bishops, mayors or head-masters, but not lawyers or politicians. The Whites in the Congo, about 100,000 of them, are given as little political power as the Africans : though some of them have settled, they are controlled firmly from Brussels. Officially there is no colour bar, but in practice the towns, hotels and cafés have been divided into Black and White, with only a few black *évolués* in the white areas.

The diversion of African discontent has been made easier, up to a point, by the discovery of enormous wealth, in the shape of copper and later uranium, in the south-east corner of the Congo, known as the *Haut Katanga*. The Belgian copper-belt makes a spectacular contrast to the Northern Rhodesian continuation of it, just across the border : in the Belgian part, Africans are allowed to perform skilled jobs, such as working cranes, mending mining engines or working machine tools : white supervisors from Belgium are carefully selected, and kept to a minimum. In Northern Rhodesia, the presence of British and Afrikaner settlers, with strong trades unions, has prevented Africans from reaching skilled employment. Since African labour is cheaper, the Belgian system is more profitable.

The Belgian system seemed in many ways remarkably successful. In the midst of the post-war surge of nationalism, the educated Congolese appeared content with economic improvement—as the French Africans seemed content with cultural achievements. Few Congolese have had access to European universities, and only since 1954 have there been two universities (one

Catholic, one Protestant) in the Congo : but they have had all the stimulus and pride of the most rapid industrial revolution in Africa, and they have formed a settled and fairly prosperous middle class with no obvious grievances. To Whites in East and Central Africa, and to many British politicians, the 'Congo solution' seemed to be the answer to nationalism. Nationalist Africans from other territories, on the rare occasions when they met the Congolese, were disappointed by their political apathy.

But several influences were working to destroy the 'Congo dream'. The Belgians themselves were rapidly becoming uneasy about their old-fashioned paternalism, and beginning to modify it. Municipal elections were held for the first time in 1958, as a first move towards the franchise, and revealed a much stronger nationalist feeling than was expected. The price of copper began falling in 1957, and with the drop came reduced imports, unemployment and anti-Belgian feeling among Africans. Perhaps most important was the formation of the Abako Movement—the Association of the People of the Lower Congo. It began as an ostensibly cultural organization of the Bacongo people, led by the mayor of one of the African townships of Leopoldville, Joseph Kazavubu—who had dreams, like the Abbé Youlou, of re-uniting the Bacongo Kingdom. But when, on the opposite bank of the Congo river, the Abbé's new Republic was proclaimed at Brazzaville, the Bacongo in Leopoldville became abruptly aware of the changes in the world outside. Brazzaville was poor, but it had votes. Fulbert and Kazavubu visited each other, and reinforced their Bacongo zeal : "We are Congolese", announced the Abbé, "on both sides of the river." On top of this new impact of nationalism came the Accra Conference at the end of 1958, attended by three delegates from the Belgian Congo, who proclaimed 'Vive l'independence Congolaise'.

From these ingredients came the first flash of Congo nationalism. On January 4, 1959—a day which has been compared for its sudden significance with Ghana's February 28—police shot at an African crowd at Leopoldville, after a meeting had been prohibited at which the delegates from the Accra Conference were to have spoken. Riots broke out in the city and spread to looting of the European shops, which lasted for four days. Police were called out and paratroops flown in from Europe to patrol the streets. Between forty (official figure) and two hundred (unofficial) Africans were killed in the resulting shooting. Ninety-six African leaders were arrested, including three mayors and Joseph Kazavubu.

But Belgium could not hope to keep down a serious nationalist movement by force, and a week later, King Baudouin, great-grandson of King Leopold, announced reforms which had been projected for several months beforehand. Though cautious and vague, they made it unequivocally clear that the Congo was now caught up in the stream of African independence. Belgium would lead, 'without fatal evasions but without imprudent haste', the Congolese peoples to 'independence in prosperity and peace'. Communal councils were to be elected by universal suffrage, a legislative council would be established, all discrimination between Black and White would be removed and a timetable for democracy would be set.

A parliamentary commission of enquiry visited the Congo to investigate the cause of the riots, and in their bold report stated that, among other factors, the trouble was caused by European segregation, the economic recession, the rapid influx of Africans into Leopoldville and the inferiority complex of African leaders, who felt that complete equality would never be reached. A month after the commission reported, the African leaders, headed by Kazavubu, who had been banished to Belgium, were returned to the Congo, and the road was opened to drastic political reforms which could only end in African self-government for the Congo.

For the white communities of Southern Africa, the riots of the Congo, coupled with the quick retreat of the Belgians, came as an end to a dream, and a frightening reminder of how quickly the whole pattern of Africa would change.

CHAPTER IV

BLACK EAST AFRICA

BETWEEN THE Congo and the Indian Ocean,
bounded on the north by Ethiopia (usually regarded
as being outside 'Black Africa'), and on the south by
Northern Rhodesia and Portuguese East Africa, are
the four territories known as British East Africa—
Kenya, Uganda, Tanganyika and the island of Zanzibar. They have a quite separate history and background to West Africa. The coastal cities from which
East Africa was developed—Mombasa, Dar-es-Salaam
or Zanzibar—have heavy layers of Arab influence.
Arab dhows still sail down with the monsoon from the
Persian Gulf every year.

Until the late nineteenth century, the Arab Sultan
on Zanzibar controlled most of the wealth of East
Africa, including the slave trade, summed up in the
famous Arab proverb: "When the flute is played in
Zanzibar, all Africa east of the Lakes must dance."
It was with the mixed motives of stamping out the
slave raids, opening up trade and converting the Africans to Christianity that the great British explorers,
following Livingstone in 1841, penetrated to the interior of East Africa between 1840 and 1880. Zanzibar
itself became a British protectorate in 1890, when the
Germans, who were also scrambling for Africa, relin-
quished their claims in exchange for the island of
Heligoland. Kenya and Uganda, having been developed
by the British East Africa Company, became British

territories four years later. At about the same time,
Tanganyika was being annexed with great efficiency by
Germany, who suppressed the 'Maji-Maji' rebellion of
1903 at the cost of 120,000 African lives. After the
First World War it became a trust territory, administered by Britain on behalf first of the League of Nations,
then of the United Nations.

The white history of East Africa is therefore very
modern, and settlement only began in the twentieth
century. There are still only 100,000 Whites in the
whole area, but by way of complication the original
pioneers imported large numbers of Indians and Goans
to help with building the railway; their descendants,
together with Asian traders and relatives who followed
them, now number over 300,000. Although small in
number compared to the twenty million Africans, they
give a strongly Asian character to many of the cities.
There are more Indians than Europeans in Mombasa
or Nairobi, and many of the shopkeepers, artisans or
even millionaires are Indian.

East Africa, particularly the high land in the interior
and the surroundings of Lake Victoria, is much more
comfortable for white settlement than the West: there
are parts of the East which are always lush, green and
temperate, with two harvests a year—like a fantasy
England. But the settlers, both white and brown, have
never been in large enough numbers to be confident
of dominating their country politically. On the other
hand the Africans—partly through the lethargy of the
governments, partly from the poverty of the territories
—have not reached the same educational level and
experience in government as the West Africans. In
1953 the average income of East Africans (including

Europeans) was £18 a year, compared to £55 in Ghana.

From this background has arisen the East African emphasis on 'multi-racialism', or 'non-racialism', as it is perhaps more happily called. Many Whites have believed that African nationalism could at least be delayed in East Africa, and that by devising 'multi-racial' constitutions, where Africans voted for Europeans and vice versa, whites could maintain their political control with the consent of Africans; and that in time the different races, with their interests interlocked, would cease to think in racial terms at all. The alternatives to multi-racialism have been summed up by a white Kenyan leader, Michael Blundell: "If you sit on them, explosion; if you give way, chaos."

The white hopes for a non-racial society were reinforced by the knowledge that, in the past, Africans in the East had been tribally-minded and divided between themselves, and that nationalism had been confused with tribalism. East Africa seemed partially protected against the waves of nationalism from the West and Centre. But the Accra Conference in December 1958, followed by the riots in the Congo, seemed to put an end to hopes of isolation. Not only has East Africa become aware of the rest of Africa: it is also ceasing to be itself four separate compartments. The influences from one to another—particularly from Tanganyika, the closest to self-government, to Kenya, the furthest from it, have become quicker and more potent.

Although they are linked together in sectors of their administration, the four territories are developing in very different directions. Kenya is still largely dominated by white settlers, while Uganda and Tanganyika are rapidly becoming African states. Zanzibar, a Moslem island with fifty thousand Arabs and two hundred thousand Africans, remains in a half-feudal condition, still ruled by a benign old Sultan, on the advice of the British 'Resident'.

*   *   *

The most 'African' of the territories, in the sense of being least affected by European intrusions, is the complex protectorate of Uganda, which rests on the top of the huge Lake Victoria—the fertile hub of East Africa. The politics of Uganda have been dominated in the past by the most populous of its four provinces, Buganda, an ancient Hamitic kingdom, after which, by a muddling nomenclature, the whole protectorate of seven million people was eventually named.

Buganda forms an astonishing exception to most of the continent: it is a tribal monarchy, in some ways similar to Northern Nigeria, which has so far survived almost intact the pressures of democracy. It has an impressive tradition of ordered rule, with even a developed civil service. The explorer Speke described in 1862 how he was first shown to the presence of the Kabaka, or King: "Courtiers of high dignity stepped forward to greet me, dressed in the most scrupulously neat fashions. Men, women, bulls, dogs and goats were led about by strings; cocks and hens were carried in men's arms; and little pages, with rope-turbans, rushed about, conveying messages, as if their lives depended on their swiftness, everyone holding his skin-cloak tightly round him lest his naked legs might by accident be shown." Later, Speke gave a carbine to the King, who loaded it and gave it to a page, telling him to shoot a man in the outer court, which he proudly did.

Speke's discovery was followed by the arrival of missionaries and by gruesome and disreputable wars between the three religious factions, Catholic, Protestant and Moslem, each competing for the favours of a corrupt monarch. But the court of the Kabaka survived these feuds, and was upheld by the British administration. Buganda is still effectively ruled by a Kabaka, the great grandson of Mutesa I, a proud and polished monarch of thirty-two, from Cambridge and the Grenadier Guards. Though nationalist movements have developed in Uganda since the war, they have not succeeded in disrupting the authority of the Kabaka and his conservative, nominated parliament, the Lukiko.

The Kabaka's position was only strengthened by a two years' exile in 1953. Alarmed by a casual reference by the Colonial Secretary to the possibility of East African Federation, the Kabaka had abruptly insisted that Buganda should be given its own programme towards full independence, quite separate, not only from the rest of East Africa, but from the rest of Uganda. In the tense talks which followed between the Kabaka and the Governor, Sir Andrew Cohen, there was not the usual African argument between a conservative governor and a popular leader, but the opposite—between a progressive governor and a conservative monarch. The Kabaka's idea of independence was of a tribal state, under his own autocratic rule. He refused to co-operate with a government which seemed bent on destroying his power; the talks broke down, and the recalcitrant King was summarily exiled to London.

But his absence united the country as never before. The young Uganda National Congress, which had been formed in 1952 with universal suffrage among its aims, joined with the Kabaka's supporters in demanding his return. The whole kingdom went into mourning, no successor was appointed, and the Kabaka's sister died of grief.

After appointing a commission, the British Government announced that they would allow the Kabaka's return—on a basis which reduced his constitutional powers—on condition that Buganda agreed to remain part of Uganda. The conditions were accepted, and it seemed that the exile might prove a disguised blessing, in easing the transition from an autocratic to a democratic state. In October 1955 the Kabaka returned to Buganda in triumph, with two plane-loads of his guests for the celebrations, to be greeted warmly by the same Governor who had exiled him.

But though his constitutional powers had been shorn, the Kabaka, like some British monarchs, succeeded in maintaining, or even increasing, his hold. The Congress, once again dedicated to overthrowing the Chiefs, was frustrated and divided by the influence of the Kabaka's court, by the workings of tradition, land, patronage, and peremptory arrests of its enemies. In contrast to Ghana or Southern Nigeria, the Baganda democratic leaders could never escape from the power of the Chieftaincy. "Imagine what it must be like", Nkrumah remarked after hearing about Buganda, "to have the capital in the middle of Ashanti."

Though Buganda was pledged to remain part of Uganda, the Kabaka's court was determined not to yield any power. When the first general elections were held for the whole of Uganda in 1958, the Lukiko resolved to take no part in them. The disunity of Uganda was further exacerbated when a section of the Congress, led by their founder-president Ignatius Musazi, split off to form a more militant Uganda National Movement in February 1959. Providing an unusual coalition, between Catholics, Protestants and Moslems, intellectuals and tribal traditionalists, the new movement seemed at first to give hope of a new unity. But after an anti-Asian boycott had led to widespread riots, the new movement was banned on May 22, Buganda was declared a disturbed area, and six leaders of the movement were rusticated.

With these frictions and internal troubles, heightened by continued religious feuds, the prospects of self-government for Uganda have become steadily more remote. Britain has stated that Uganda shall become an African state as soon as possible: but the Kabaka's government rejects any notion of leaving Uganda in the hands of African voters. It may ironically be part of Uganda's difficulty that there are only ten thousand European settlers, with very limited rights. The fact that neither Britain nor British immigrants have provided an obstacle to self-government has made it harder for Uganda nationalists to unite.

*   *   *

Below Uganda, and four times its size, lies Tanganyika, second in area among British territories only to Nigeria. It is a sleepier country than Uganda. Its nine million people come from a hundred different tribes—including one of the grandest, most untouched

tribes in Africa, the Masai—with no central stronghold like the Kabaka's court. Its capital, the lazy port
of Dar-es-Salaam, has little of the vigour of Kampala.
Education is less widespread, and there are only 3,000
children at secondary schools. The 21,000 white
settlers are more evident, together with nearly 80,000
Asians.

Tanganyika has appeared as one of the happiest, most
tolerant territories in Africa, almost unaffected by the
Mau Mau to the north, or the nationalism to the
south. Since the war it has been governed under the
benign, easy-going control of the Colonial Office, with
the Governor holding a balance in the Legislative
Council between the Whites, Africans and Asians.

But in spite of its apparent lethargy, Tanganyika
now seems likely to be the first East African territory
to reach independence. The Tanganyikans have had
two major advantages. Firstly, they are under United
Nations trusteeship, subject to inspection every three
years from visiting UN missions. While often prais-
ing the administrators, the United Nations have con-
tinually pressed—to the annoyance of the British—for
a *timetable* for political independence, and have never
let the Africans forget their birthright. But even the
UN timetables have been quickly outdated by the
pace of African aspirations: in 1954 the UN demanded a promise of independence within twenty years
—a deadline which would now seem absurdly distant.

But a greater asset to the Africans is the single personality of their unchallenged leader, Julius Nyerere.
He is an unusual type of African leader—a quiet ex-
schoolmaster of only thirty-eight, graduated from Edinburgh University, with a neat ivory walking-stick and a

trim British moustache which is copied by many educated Tanganyikans. He is courteous, humorous, quite
unbitter, and gives Africans the impression of being very
British. Since he founded the Tanganyika African
National Union (TANU) in 1954, he has built it up
into one of the most efficient and disciplined political
bodies in British Africa, with an estimated half a million members. The face of Nyerere looks out from por-
traits, posters, match-boxes and the local newspaper,
Mwafrika. In a territory where highly-educated Africans are still rare, he enjoys the simple prestige of the
man with Western experience, and he has the advantage of a common language, Swahili, through most of
the territory. The Colonial Government have provided
just enough opposition to TANU—bans, fines, restrictions and prosecutions—to give it unity and enthusiasm,
without enough to seriously impede it. Most of all,
Nyerere has succeeded by steadily obeying the advice
which Nkrumah gives to all African leaders : organize,
organize, organize.

In September 1958 the first general elections were
held in the territory, with an ingenious 'tripartite' system of franchise designed to favour non-racial voting :
each elector of every race was required to vote for
three candidates, one African, one White, one Asian.
Unlike Kenya, where voting has always been on a
communal basis, with Whites voting for Whites and
Blacks for Blacks, Tanganyika went straight to a common roll, with multi-racial voters electing multi-racial
members. The theory of the system was that, since
black candidates would have to appeal to Whites and
vice versa, the teeth would be taken out of nationalist
policies.

But the result of this experiment was not quite so raceless. TANU, controlling the majority of voters, sponsored candidates of all three races. All thirty of the elected members—five of each race—were sponsored by TANU: so that, although the parliament was pleasantly multi-coloured, they all represented the same political power—the power of African nationalism.

There was nothing racialistic about Nyerere's policies, and he has always recognized the rights and usefulness of Whites and Asians: indeed, his opponent, Zuberi Mtemvu, the leader of the extremist Tanganyika African National Congress advocating 'Africa for Africans only', has accused him of subjugating Africans to White and Asian domination. But as Africans became more confident of their future, the appeal of racialism became less.

But the independence of Tanganyika presents much graver problems than that of Ghana. The speed of her change has left her with few qualified black administrators. Moreover, the fact that Ghana simultaneously achieved political independence and economic independence—through cocoa—has often misled other Africans. Tanganyika is still dependent on a British subsidy, and without paying her own way her independence, like Liberia's, would be superficial. With growing anxiety, the Tanganyikans—who have already been twice disappointed since the war by the collapse of the ground-nuts scheme and the fall in sisal prices—are looking to the oil and mineral prospectors, and to the diamond mines, to provide the wealth with which to make their independence real.

The blackness of Tanganyika, alongside Uganda,

has a special geographical meaning, for it forms a huge wedge between two white-dominated areas—Rhodesia and Kenya. It will particularly affect the white community of Kenya, isolated in the middle of a ring of black countries growing to independence.

CHAPTER V

KENYA

KENYA, THOUGH IT has only 65,000 Whites to
six million Africans, is a country where the white man
has made himself felt. Its capital, Nairobi, in immediate contrast to Dar-es-Salaam or Kampala, is more
like an English suburb, with trim hedges, well-kept
green verges, and neat brick houses reminiscent of the
Surrey hills. The English aristocracy of Kenya has in
the past been legendary for its luxury, eccentricity,
wildness and enterprise, forming a kind of residue of
Empire: they include refugees from British India,
many of whom left in disgust even before independence. But since the last war Kenya immigrants have
been more prosaic, respectable and commercial.

Where Nairobi is not English, it is Indian. There
are 170,000 Indians in the colony, outnumbering the
whites three to one. In Nairobi most of the stores,
cinemas, garages belong to Indians, giving a gaudy
Asian fringe to the English centre. The existence of
this large Indian middle class has separated Whites
still further from the African majority: the Indians
have in the past both underpinned the white way of
life, and excluded Africans from more responsible jobs.

But the crux of the African's complaint, as elsewhere, is not jobs, but land. Since Lord Delamere, the
first white settler, was granted 100,000 acres in the
White Highlands of Kenya in 1903, British immigrants soon discovered that this rich, high land was

some of the best in the world. The Africans, particularly the large and clever Kikuyu tribe, found themselves
excluded from the best land, which, however fitful their
own use of it had been, they regarded as their own.
The exclusive Whiteness of the White Highlands remains the most burning grievance of the Kenya
Africans.

Ever since the first settlements, the British Government has been uncertain about the relative political
rights of Whites and Blacks in a colony with such a
small but influential white community. The ambiguity
came to a head as early as 1923, when the Conservative
Colonial Secretary, the Duke of Devonshire, made the
famous statement that 'the interests of the African
natives must be paramount, and that if and when those
interests and the interests of the immigrant races should
conflict, the former should prevail'.

But the power and the richest land remained white,
and the resulting African land hunger and frustration,
together with a crude and arrogant colour bar, led in-
exorably to the Mau Mau rebellion of 1952, which
changed the face of Kenya. The White's survival of
the rebellion, in which fifty-three Europeans and
twenty thousand Africans were killed, was due to one
overriding factor. The revolt was restricted not only
to one tribe, the Kikuyu, but to only part of the tribe,
and the crushing of the rebellion was largely due to
the 'loyalist' Kikuyu who joined with the British forces.
While most Africans, in and out of Kenya, regarded
the Mau Mau as a justifiable revolt against intolerable
privations, it was too tribal, retrogressive and exclusive
to be regarded as a national movement. The Kikuyu,
by far the ablest tribe in Kenya, have a passion for

tribal movements and secret societies, which antagonizes the others. The Mau Mau, though it is often invoked by Whites in other parts of Africa, has no real parallel elsewhere, and can only be fully explained in Kikuyu terms.

While the murders themselves were a tribal movement, discontent was national. The anger of all the Kenya tribes was expressed in the glittering personality of Jomo Kenyatta, the Kikuyu intellectual who laid the basis of revolt. Kenyatta, though now banished indefinitely to the barren Northern Province of Kenya, still haunts Kenya as a symbol of African strength and unity. He returned to Kenya after seventeen years abroad in 1946, just before his friend Nkrumah returned to the Gold Coast. His fiery, bearded presence brought all the excitement of post-war nationalism to the Kikuyu. His trial in 1952, and sentence of seven years for managing the Mau Mau, has since been strongly criticized; but whatever his implication with the Mau Mau, it is clear that (like Makarios in Cyprus) he could have stopped it, and did not.

The memory of the Mau Mau still dominates Kenya politics and policies. Though the last shot was fired in 1955, the 'Emergency' still continues, permitting immense police powers; iron control of the Kikuyu through curfews, passes and permits; restrictions on all African political parties; and indefinite detention without trial of about a thousand suspects. Some of the outrageous abuses of these extreme powers came to light in the enquiry into the deaths of eleven detainees at Hola Camp on March 6, 1959, following attempts to force them to work by beating. But the most important effect of the rebellion has been its impact on the white minority, whose confidence and insulation could never be the same again. It is one of the ugliest lessons of Africa that the murders of the Mau Mau achieved a change of thinking among Europeans unthinkable in peacetime. While the British Government gave 28 million pounds and lent three battalions to Kenya, it was clear that the tiny white minority could not hope to stay in Kenya by force.

The liberalization of Kenya after the Mau Mau, inadequate though it may seem, was one of the most sudden changes in colonial history. In 1954 the British Colonial Secretary, Oliver Lyttleton, put forward a new multi-racial constitution which the local settlers, being defended by British troops, were in no position to reject. It allowed much greater non-White participation in Government—including one African and two Indian ministers—and led to the first African general elections in 1956, when eight African members were elected. In the post-Mau Mau years, the idea of 'multiracialism', which before the emergency had been unmentionable by white politicians, became accepted as the last hope for the survival of the settlers. The social colour bar was rapidly and visibly relaxed : Africans and Indians were admitted, and even welcomed, into hotels and restaurants, and acquaintance with Africans became a political asset. The old Kenya had vanished.

But the change was not rapid or drastic enough for the Africans, who had gathered a new confidence from the ballot-box, from the emergence of Black Africa all round them, and from the evident weakness of the white front. While the Mau Mau, and the subsequent restrictions on politics, was often an embarrassment to

the new leaders, it was also an advantage, for it gave
a sense of unity. At the head of the new nationalism
was a handsome, highly intelligent young Luo (a
neighbouring, but much less active, tribe to the
Kikuyu), Tom Mboya, who was only twenty-eight
when he was first elected to parliament in 1956.
Mboya, trained as a trade unionist and thoroughly
detribalized, was a much more modern leader than
Kenyatta, with none of his tribal obscurantism. He
was determined to achieve African independence in
Kenya with strictly Western weapons: his shrewdness,
urbanity and ability to outwit his white opponents
captured a black electorate who were tiring of tribalism.

The objections of Mboya were not only that Africans were not sufficiently represented in parliament,
but that they were represented in the wrong way—
by a communal roll, not a common one. It was one of
the most dangerous features of the Kenya parliament,
ever since the first Indians were elected in 1923, that
the races were divided by separate rolls, with Whites
electing Whites, Indians Indians, and later Africans
Africans. These communal rolls, an inheritance from
India, inevitably sharpened the racial conflicts, and
produced white and black leaders who made political
capital out of attacking each other. White ministers,
elected by Whites to represent their interests, could
not hope to be impartial in their administration. It was,
in the words of one European minister, 'like having
the Chancellor of the Exchequer appointed by the
Stock Exchange'.

In the three years after 1954, the initiative in Kenya
passed from the Whites to Africans. The Whites, know-
ing that they could not govern Kenya by themselves,

but divided as to the measure of multi-racialism, fell into splinters and recriminations. Whereas in 1954 it had been the Africans who sought the protection of the Colonial Office, three years later it was the Whites who, having previously thrived on talk of 'Boston Tea Parties', now begged London to protect them from black nationalism. The turning-point, in the view of Africans, came in 1957 when, after general election had been held for Africans, the elected black members refused to accept a place in the Government. Their boycott successfully undermined the Lyttelton Constitution, which was dissolved. The fact that African leaders could force the hand of the Government, by making the constitution unworkable, added tremendously to their confidence.

After a period of unsuccessful negotiations between the races, a new 'Lennox-Boyd Constitution' was devised, which allowed six more seats to the Africans, in place of the fifteen they had demanded, but kept firm white control of the Government. It also arranged for twelve 'specially elected' members, three of each race, to be elected by members of parliament—a system which was hoped to provide a way out of the rut of the communal rolls. But the African members boycotted the special seats on the grounds that they would provide 'stooge Africans', and later boycotted the Legislative Council altogether. The empty African seats in parliament became a constant reminder of the non-co-operation of Africans.

The crux of the argument between Whites and Africans was, of course, whether Kenya was to become an African state. The Whites in April 1959 formed a new multi-racial party under one of their most realistic

members, the bluff Yorkshire farmer Michael Blundell, who was committed to two bold moves, admitting
Africans into the White Highlands, and the beginning
of a common roll. The party was welcomed by most
Whites as a 'last chance' to save Kenya from the 'waves
of rampant racialism' : but although it had the majority
of Whites behind it, the party included no African
elected member, and in its manifesto there was no
mention of the word which interested Africans most,
democracy. It was implicit in the policy of the new
party that they were opposed to majority rule. The
formation of Blundell's party did succeed in encouraging a split among the hitherto united African MP's,
some of whom joined in July 1959 a new interracial
'Kenya National Party', with more moderate attributes
than Mboya's, though more militant than Blundell's.

Mboya's group demanded nothing less than genuine
British democracy. It was clear, as Uganda and Tanganyika moved forward, that Kenya must eventually
become an African state—an admission made privately
by the British government. But, with the races stuck
in their communal grooves, the change-over would be
a hard and painful one. It was suggested by some
liberals that only the reversion of Kenya to full control
from London for a period of years could change the
pattern of racial attitudes : but the Africans, having
once tasted power, were unlikely to abdicate it, however temporarily.

Kenya will be the key to East Africa's future. Richer,
more disciplined and developed than her neighbours,
she has reaped all the advantages of white settlement,
and has survived the Mau Mau disaster with astonishing resilience. Nairobi is the financial capital of East

Africa, with a tradition and climate which the others have not. Whether the white settlers—who now regard themselves as the underdogs of Africa—can adjust themselves to living in a black Kenya is as important to Africans as it is to themselves.

CHAPTER VI

PORTUGUESE AFRICA

THE LEAST-KNOWN territories in Africa are the
Spanish and Portuguese, of which the latter are far
the largest. Spain, apart from Morocco and Spanish
Sahara in the North, has only the cocoa island of
Fernando Po—the island from which cocoa was first
imported to Ghana in 1870—and the barren coastal
settlement of Rio Muni, which was colonized from it.
Fernando Po is mainly known for the allegations which
have been and still are made against it, of obtaining
forced labour from Liberia and latterly from Nigeria.

Portuguese Africa consists of the small bit of Portuguese Guinea in the West Coast, and of two huge slabs
known as Portuguese East and West Africa—or Mozambique and Angola—separated in the middle by the
Rhodesias. Of the two, the East is superficially better
known, for it contains the two ports of Beira and
Lourenço Marques, the main outlets for Rhodesia and
the gold-mines of South Africa. They have exciting
modern architecture, luxurious hotels and gay, shabby
bars which seem exaggeratedly Continental after the
uniformity of Johannesburg and Salisbury. But the
cars, machinery or bars of copper at the docks, and
the extravagance of the hotels, point to the fact that
the towns—the two biggest in Mozambique—live
largely off the freight and tourism from South and
Central Africa. Angola, similarly, is the vital outlet
from the Congo to the Atlantic.

Though both colonies originated in the sixteenth century, it is only in the last hundred years that they have been fully colonized, after the independence of Brazil deprived Lisbon of its principal possession. By 1907 the Portuguese Government had begun to give Mozambique the first steps towards self-government. But this trend was reversed under the new totalitarian régime of 1926, which, being desperately short of money, could not afford to let go its African possessions. Since then Portuguese Africa, much more than French or even Spanish Africa, has come to be regarded as part of Portugal, with strong governors responsible to Lisbon. Without democracy in the home country, there has been little incentive to grant it in the colonies.

What little has been discovered about the methods adopted in Portuguese Africa is not pleasant. The first major investigation was conducted by the British journalist H. W. Nevinson in 1905, who was sent out by *Harper's Magazine* to investigate allegations of slavery. His book, *A Modern Slavery*, and the reports of later investigators, revealed the large-scale use of forced labour, in conditions hardly distinguishable from slavery. Fifty years later *Harper's* sent another British journalist, Basil Davidson, on the same enquiry. His report in his book, *The African Awakening*, together with reports from the Anti-Slavery Society and the International Labour Office, suggest that the abuses of 'contract labour' or *contradados* are still widespread. Nearly half the labour force of Angola, according to Davidson, is still made up by *contradados*, as opposed to *voluntarios* (379,000 to 420,000). *Contradados* are obtained by the local *Chefe de Posto*, who provides them either from tax-defaulters or by pressure on the local Chief : it is said that in many cases the Portuguese officials were heavily bribed to produce contract labourers. The workers on the cocoa fields of the island of São Tomé are still—as they were in the time of Nevinson—largely obtained from the forced labour of deported Africans. A Captain Galvao, who was sent by the Portuguese Government in 1947 to report on labour conditions, and later secretly circulated a highly critical report, was sentenced in 1958 to sixteen years' imprisonment after a secret trial.

Though the Portuguese angrily deny the charges of forced labour, and maintain that the contract recruits are voluntary, they make no bones about the harshness of their treatment of offenders. The stern discipline imposed on domestic servants is the envy of many white South Africans. For a minor theft they are beaten,˙ for a second offence often deported without trace : as a result, labour relations are, for the Portuguese, very docile. The severity of the methods is testified by the mass emigrations of Africans.

To offset their treatment of the masses, the Portuguese have, like the French, Belgians and Spanish, a system of *assimilados*, or 'civilized' Africans, who are allowed the same rights and privileges as the Portuguese. With their own long contact with the Moors, and with a long tradition of intermarriage, the Portuguese have probably less emotional sense of colour bar than any European nation in Africa : the few educated Africans from South Africa who cross to Mozambique are astonished to find themselves welcomed by the Portuguese with intimacy or even seductions. If an African can satisfy a tribunal that he leads a European

way of life without native customs, that he can speak
and write Portuguese, can earn a moderate living and
has completed military service, he can in theory become an *assimilado*, and make use of European courts,
schools, hotels or houses. The system, as elsewhere,
has removed the leaders from their people and creates
a favourable impression on visitors. But the last figures
(1950) for the numbers of *assimilados* showed only
241,000 in the Portuguese territories, out of a population of ten million.

The iron control of the colonies from Lisbon, the
strict barriers against outside influences, and the tech-
nique of the *assimilados* have all protected Portuguese
Africa from the nationalism elsewhere. But from the
leaks of news there are signs that *assimilados* are beginning to share the sense of agitation, and the desire
to organize their people. At the same time the local
settlers are chafing at the control from Lisbon. Although
the Portuguese, as in Goa, have shown unusual tenacity
in retaining their colonies, it seems doubtful if these
fortresses can indefinitely withstand the pressures of
the rest of Africa.

CHAPTER VII

SOUTH AFRICA

To fly from West Africa to South Africa—a distance of thirteen hours—is like visiting the opposite end of the world. There is nothing except the black faces—and even they are lighter and more Western-looking—to suggest that they are in the same continent. After the African states in the north, South Africa seems irrelevant, and utterly separate. The three million Whites, though only a quarter of the African population, dominate the cities so obviously that South Africa seems closer to Europe or America. The white newspapers give much more prominence to news from New York or London than from Accra or Leopold-ville: few passengers break their journey between South Africa and Europe. Historically, economically and psychologically, white South Africa is a European appendage cut off from Africa. To Africans, shut out by lack of passports and news from the north, its frontiers are an iron curtain.

Though Cape Town has the parliament, and Pretoria the administration, the nerve-centre of the Union is Johannesburg, the seventy-year-old 'Golden City' from which most of its wealth comes. Johannesburg, second only in population to Cairo, is by far the wealthiest city in Africa: with its bony skyscrapers, traffic jams of American cars, and surroundings of green, watered suburbs with tennis courts and swimming pools, it has all the appearance of an American

—particularly a Texan—city. Johannesburg makes every capital to the north look petty, and it points to the fact that South Africa has more industry than the rest of Black Africa put together.

The isolation of South Africa is implicit in its history. It was founded when an official of the Dutch East India Company, Jan Van Riebeck, established a revictualling base at Cape Town, on the route to India, on June 26, 1653—a day commemorated by white celebrations and black protests. The fact that settlement has existed for three hundred years helps to make white South African attitudes much firmer and more uncompromising than those of Kenya or Rhodesia. The descendants of the first Dutch settlers, who called themselves 'Afrikaners', became mixed with English colonists after the Cape was occupied by Britain in 1795: the British remained in the two coastal colonies of the Cape and Natal, while the Afrikaners later trekked to establish the two northern republics of the Orange Free State and Transvaal.

After the bitter defeat of the Afrikaners in the Boer War in 1902 the two colonies and the two republics were eventually welded together—in a remarkable act of reconciliation—in the new self-governing Union of 1910. But this act of liberalism to the Afrikaners was made at the expense of the Africans, who had no vote in the new state, except in the Cape Province. It was the hope of the British Government at the time that the Boer provinces in the north would gradually be liberalized by the British provinces, and that the African vote would be extended. But the Liberals of 1910 were too preoccupied with being fair to Afrikaners to be fair to Africans too: and the new constitution left the Africans feeling betrayed and forsaken by Britain.

The new Union remained largely dominated by the British, and Afrikaner nationalism continued to burn fiercely, still fired by the humiliation of the Boer War. South Africa has suffered two overlapping revolutions —the revolt of Afrikaners against the British and the revolt of Africans against the Whites. Up till the last war, the main 'problem' of South Africa was of Afrikaners, not Africans, and 'nationalism' meant Afrikaner nationalism. Not until 1948, when the United Party of General Smuts was defeated by the 'pure' Afrikaner party of Dr. Malan, did the Afrikaner nationalists believe that they had won the last battle of the Boer War. With two-thirds of the white population Afrikaner, and the votes loaded in their favour, the age of 'Afrikanerdom'—as they called their ideal state—had dawned.

But although the Afrikaners have maintained firm political control for the past ten years, the English-speaking population, with their cosmopolitan connections, have continued to wield the economic power— particularly the gold, uranium and diamond mines which provide most of South Africa's exports. The resentment of Afrikaners against this economic domination, together with their growing fear of the black four-fifths of the population, have maintained the impetus and bitterness of their nationalism.

Among the non-Europeans there are almost equal complications. Apart from the twelve million Africans, divided into four main tribes, there are 400,000 Indians, many of them descended from the indentured labourers in the sugar-fields of Natal, who hover unhappily between Western ambitions and African disabilities. There are a million 'Coloureds', as half-castes are called in South Africa, the product of three hundred years of miscegenation who, like the Indians, have found themselves steadily and reluctantly pressed towards the Africans. Within the racial communities there are divisions between light-skinned and dark-skinned, Hindu or Moslem, traders or labourers, which all add to the racial turmoil of the country.

But these divisions between non-Europeans are gradually fading in the face of the overpowering Afrikaner policy of *apartheid*, or separateness of the races.

There is nothing specifically Afrikaner about the idea of segregation, which has been implied in the policies of all white Governments, English or Afrikaner, since Union in 1910. Restrictive laws against Africans, beginning with the Land Act of 1913, were passed by both English and Afrikaner governments, and the abolition of the African vote, which was affected in 1936, was supported by a nearly united parliament. Even since 1948, the opposition from the predominantly English United Party has been fitful and often hypocritical—preferring to criticize the details rather than the principles of *apartheid*. The three most drastic laws suppressing civil liberties, the Suppression of Communism Act (1950), and the Public Safety and Criminal Law Amendment Acts (1953), were all supported by both sides of the House.

Afrikaners often claim that *apartheid* is nothing more than a term, in the words of their Foreign Minister, with a "softer and less stringent connotation than the word 'segregation' used in the United States". But *apartheid* is in fact much harder, with all the sternness of Calvinism behind it, in the extreme form of the Afrikaners' Dutch Reformed Church. *Apartheid*

is not simply a social custom; it is a passionate belief
in the evils of racial mixing, and of the chosen mission
of the white man. It derives from the brave and lonely
history of the Afrikaner people, forging a place for
themselves with Bible, rifle and ox-wagon, still the
symbols of their race. But it is not only Calvinism and
isolation which distinguishes *apartheid* from British or
American segregation. It is, more than anything else,
the knowledge by Afrikaners that they have no other
home, and that they have long ago cut their roots from
Europe.

It is the desperation, the heroic and perhaps sui-
cidal element of *apartheid*, which makes South Africa
a special case in Africa. Just at the time when African
nationalism was beginning to boil over in the continent, South Africa passed into the hands of a Government which was determined to withstand it.

This intractability is personified in the Prime Minister, Dr. Hendrik Verwoerd, a tall, boyish-looking
professor of fifty-eight. The son, not of an Afrikaner,
but a Hollander, he has consistently outbidden his
colleagues by the extremity of his views, and with a
hard, academic intellect he has been prepared to take
apartheid to its logical conclusions—even to the unusual extent of having no African servants in his home.
After studying at German universities, he became at
twenty-eight Professor of Applied Philosophy at the
Afrikaner University of Stellenbosch, which remains
the stronghold of Afrikaner intellectuals. He became
intimately concerned with the nationalist struggle, and
nine years later was Editor of the daily *Die Transvaler*
in Johannesburg, a violent opponent of the British, and
supporter of the Nazis during the war years. His

single-minded vision and immense enthusiasm earned
him the post of Minister of Native Affairs in 1950,
where for eight years he set about the gigantic problem
of segregation and control which his predecessors had
evaded. He had no doubts about the rightness of his
mission : he saw himself as the Chief above all Chiefs,
chosen to lead the Bantu people to a happier and less
bewildered world.

*   *   *

For many of the rural Chiefs, bound to the Government by their salary, this role was acceptable. There
remains in parts of South Africa a feudal bond between Africans and Afrikaner who, having shared the
country for a hundred years or more, have reached an
understanding much warmer than that between Englishmen and Africans; for the patriarchal Afrikaner
farmer in the country is himself half-African in his
warm and hospitable life.

But the old order of South Africa was first broken
in 1867, when diamonds were discovered in Kimberley, and in 1886, when gold was found near Johannesburg. 'The Rand', as the chain of gold-mines is called,
was the foundation of modern South Africa : from its
gold came not only three billion pounds in the following seventy years, but the network of towns, ports and
railways around which secondary industry and a large
urban population conglomerated. Gold shattered the
old society, both of the Afrikaner and the African
people : they poured into the cities, detribalized and
bewildered, to form the new industrial middle and
working class.

This industrialization, as much as the presence of
three million whites, has made the Africans in South

Africa a very different people from those further north. Around three million Africans now live in towns, while the remainder either work on farms or live in the reserves. The gold and diamond mines themselves employ mainly 'contract labour', a system by which African men are recruited from the reserves, taken to the mines for a year or eighteen months, and then sent back to their families. But the servants, factory-workers, messengers or dustmen—the workers in fact in all jobs which the white men avoid—are all Africans. They form more than half the urban population, and there are now as many town Africans as the total white population. Most of the urban Africans were born urban, and in South Africa the 'men of two worlds' have often become men of one world—the world of the cities. They live in the most intensively industrialized region of the continent.

Industry has transformed black South Africans. They have become Westernized by all the machines of the West—trains, clocks, wage-packets, cinemas, rush-hours, juke-boxes, alcohol, police. To many black Cockneys, the world of the Chiefs, witch-doctors and tribal councils is as remote as it is to Europeans. Their mass uprooting is probably the most drastic operation of its kind outside Russia and China.

Above this education of the streets has been the education of the schools. Since the first English and Scots missionary outposts were established in the nineteenth century, the schooling of Africans has developed, in the wake of the new wealth, into a system with—as the Whites proudly claim—the highest *per capita* expenditure in the continent. Until the Bantu Education Act of 1954, African education was essentially Western, with the liberalizing influences of Tom Paine, Shelley, Adam Smith or Dickens.

This is the central paradox of South Africa. The country which insists most rigidly on the separation and subjection of the African people has also produced the most sophisticated, thoughtful and urbanized Africans in the continent—experienced in everything except the tools of power. In South Africa, Western civilization has not just touched the edge of African life as it has in Kenya or Rhodesia : it has enveloped it.

The sudden rush of Africans to the cities has made the task of controlling them much harder. The structure of discriminating laws in South Africa, beginning with the Land Act, which allows the African three-quarters only 13 per cent of the land, is firm enough : long before the Afrikaner Nationalist Government came into power, there were laws to prevent Africans from competing with white skilled labour, from forming trades unions, from living in the cities without permission or passes. Ever since Cecil Rhodes required cheap, tame labour for his diamond-mines, a system of taxes, passes and permits has been devised to ensure that African workers can be directed and disciplined.

But the pace of industry played havoc with these controls. The system of segregation may have been in the first place no harsher than in the Southern States of America : but while in America the ambitious Negroes left for the freedom of the cities in the North, South Africa had Harlem in its midst. Africans swarmed into the towns, building shack-towns, living off their wits, creating along the Rand the biggest black metropolis in the continent. Black writers, head-masters, doctors, university lecturers or jazz musicians lived next to gangsters, messengers or factory workers. With the shortage of white labour, employers turned more and more to black workers, even in skilled jobs.

It was against this higgledy-piggledy background that the Nationalist Government set about devising its grand new pattern of *apartheid*. In the years following 1948 a whole series of new acts were put forward to arrange that this black flood would not only be held back, but pushed back. Pass laws were tightened, and extended to women. The Group Areas Act (1950) was passed, to cut cities into racial sections. The Bantu Authorities Act (1951) bolstered the powers of the Chiefs—the allies of the Government against the masses. The Natives Resettlement Act (1954) authorized the removal of 70,000 Africans from the muddled centre of Johannesburg. The Native Laws Amendment Act (1957) made social meetings between Whites and Blacks, even in Church, a punishable offence. Most far-reaching of all, the Bantu Education Act (1955) removed the control of African education from the missionaries to the Government, and provided a special syllabus to train Africans along tribal, not Western lines, and to ensure—in the words of Dr. Verwoerd—that 'there is no place for the Native in European Society above certain forms of labour'. To follow it, the Extension of University Education Bill (1959) brought to an end the admission of Africans to White Universities, and authorized the creation of new tribal African colleges.

In some respects this programme was simply a drastic rationalization of an old South African anomaly. For decades, Africans had with the one hand been taught to admire the democracy of the West, to appreciate Western writers, humanists and philosophers, while with the other hand they had been denied all the fruits of their learning and, having left school, been pushed back into segregated squalor. The new Government, recognizing this discrepancy, decided to condition Africans to their lowly station, and to direct them, in the words of a famous South African cliché, to 'develop along their own lines'. To many Afrikaners this policy is more than a convenience : it is a faith. They love the chiefly, tribal African as much as they hate the detribalized 'cheeky Kaffir'. They believe that Africans would be happier in their separate world, as the Old Testament had ordained.

To Africans, however, this idealistic vision appears only in the form of mass arrests, new restrictions, pass-raids and wholesale removals. They have no wish to retreat to a tribal state, even if they believe the Government's promises : their lives have been built in the white men's cities, and it is there that they wish to stay.

Yet the militant African opposition to white supremacy had been slow in growing, and to Africans elsewhere the black South Africans seem submissive and moderate. One reason is obvious : the Africans face a far more determined Government, and a much larger white population, than anywhere south of Algeria. But the more important cause is the lack of nationalistic feeling. Since the final conquest in 1879 of the Zulu nation—the strongest of the South African tribes—the Africans have been deracinated and confused by the wonders of the West. The new African middle class in the towns have been too preoccupied with their salary, house and status to take the risks of politics, while the proletariat have been divided and bewildered by the struggle for existence. Though many Africans retain tribal loyalties, they have no strong tribal pride such as exists in Kenya or Nigeria. They have seen too much of the West to want to return to their roots. African leaders cannot stir up enthusiasm for the old Africa before the white man came, as they have in Ghana or Nigeria: there is nothing that the black South African wants less than to return to the bleak past of beads, mats and mud huts. With their close contact with the West, they are—like American Negroes—much less sure of themselves than the nationalists from the black North. "When you've been told you're inferior for three hundred years," a young African writer said to me, "it's difficult not to believe it."

For these reasons, the development of African politics has been fitful. The main black political body, the African National Congress, was founded as early as 1912 as a protection against the new Union, which Africans dreaded and distrusted. But their first attempts at mass action, strikes or the burning of passes were frustrated by police reprisals, tribal divisions, and the schism between the Chiefs, the intellectuals, and the workers. Three milestones mark the growth of African unity. The first was the abolition of the African vote in 1936, which, although it affected only 11,000 voters in the Cape, embittered the educated Africans, who had till then been separated from the masses by the hope of white privileges. After their vote had gone, many of them turned to Congress and action outside parliament. The second was the war, which gave Africans a glimpse of a freer, fairer world. The third was the arrival of Dr. Malan in 1948, which slammed the doors in the faces of Africans, and finally ended their prospects of entry into the white world. Intellectuals, bourgeoisie and factory workers were all pressed back into the same narrow front.

While Africans in the North were shouting 'Freedom', 'Self-government Now', or 'One Man, One Vote', Congress in South Africa was fighting desperately against the flood of laws. Soon after the Nationalist Government came to power in 1948, a more militant wing of Congress took over, based on the 'Youth League'—though still much less militant than movements further north. They planned and executed in 1953 a passive resistance campaign for the defiance of 'six unjust laws'. In six months eight thousand Africans and Indians, together with a handful of white sympathizers, went to jail for deliberately flouting permit regulations. The Government replied with the full force of its powers, by passing two Acts in January 1954 which effectively prohibited any passive resistance or encouragement of it, with penalties up to five lashes and five years in jail.

A further climax came three years later when, after Congress had organized a 'Congress of the People' to approve a mildly-worded 'Freedom Charter', the Government arrested 156 Congress leaders on a charge of treason. The trials, which after two and a half years are still in progress at the time of writing, became one of the dullest and most eccentric proceedings in legal history. With a cross-section of Africans in the dock from a professor to a bus-driver, they pointed dramatically to the impasse between black leaders and white.

The tragedy of the African impasse was exemplified in the career of their sixty-year-old leader, Albert

Luthuli, the President of Congress, who was arrested
for treason and later discharged. He is a rugged Zulu
chief whose whole career had been inspired by Christian teaching, and who had tried devotedly to follow
a moderate path. As a young man he had been a mission school-teacher, regarded by his militant con-
temporaries as a 'mission boy' or stooge, and he was
later elected to a chieftaincy in a mission reserve. But,
after watching his people's rights being whittled away,
he turned to an active role in the passive resistance
campaign of 1953, and was ordered by the Government to resign his chieftaincy or resign from Congress.
In his reply to the Government, reaffirming his militant
role in Congress, he expressed the feelings of many of
his generation :

> "Who will deny that thirty years of my life have
> been spent knocking in vain, patiently, moderately
> and modestly at a closed and barred door? What
> have been the fruits of moderation? The past thirty
> years have seen the greatest number of laws restrict-
> ing our rights and progress until today we have
> reached a stage where we have almost no rights
> at all."

Luthuli and most of his colleagues in Congress
continued to advocate cautious and largely negative
policies, with insistence on non-violence and non-
racialism. Though Congress was assisted and occasionally exploited by a small body of white communists—
the only whites who were prepared to ally themselves
with African nationalists—there was little suggestion
of communism within Congress itself. The danger that

Congress faced was not communism but racialism, and as Afrikaner racialism became more ruthless, so it seemed inevitable that Africans should adopt a counter-colour-bar. Luthuli's multi-racialism came under increasing fire from the right wing of Congress, who eventually in 1958 split off angrily to form their own group of 'Africanists', as they called themselves, adopting the old slogan of 'Africa for the Africans'. The Africanists accused the Congress leaders of selling out to left-wing Whites and Indians, and of betraying the pure African soul of Congress. The more desperate Africans become, the more they seem likely to turn to the Africanists : "When it comes to the shooting", one of them said, "the people will only see black."

In this predicament, the small courageous group of white liberals find themselves sadly isolated. Their Liberal Party had taken the bold step of advocating universal suffrage as the only solution, and had accumulated some African following. But their prospects of power seemed tiny, and most political Africans were more inclined to take their own steps towards power.

Meanwhile, the Afrikaner Government, noticing the changes in the rest of Africa and becoming unhappily aware of the necessity of co-existing with them, had begun to extend *apartheid* to give the appearance of self-governing African states within the Union, to be known as 'Bantustans'—while abolishing the existing 'Natives' Representatives' in parliament. These tribal states would, they argue, be 'in keeping' with developments in the north. The Promotion of Bantu Self-Government Bill, passed in June 1959, was the first step in providing this 'New Look', as Ministers called it, to *apartheid.* But the races in South Africa have become so tightly interlocked that the cost of a fair separation would be enormous: a preliminary scheme for developing existing African areas put forward by the Tomlinson Report in 1955 called for £130 million, and was quickly shelved. So long as Africans can own only 13 per cent of the land, no 'Bantustan' can be acceptable to them. Their areas are only ink-spots on the map of South Africa, and land remains their first and last demand.

Though still many years off, there seems little hope of averting an eventual head-on clash between the two competing nationalisms, African and Afrikaner. Whether the Afrikaners will face this Nemesis, or eventually yield to the flood, is still unknown. So far their Government has faced little formidable opposition, either from Africans or Europeans, to their policies. The pressure of world opinion has not yet taken the form of sanctions, and in diplomacy and defence South Africa is still supported by Britain and America as a vital ally against communism. Only in the last three years has the flow of foreign capital to the Union stopped, and the full cost of *apartheid* begun to show itself. It is still possible that, facing a united African opposition and world pressure, the South African Government may change its course.

CHAPTER VIII

THE OTHER SOUTH AFRICA

THE BLATANT RACIAL policies of South Africa
have caused embarrassments and problems all round
its long frontiers. But for no countries have they been
more alarming than for the curious group of three
British protectorates, Bechuanaland, Swaziland and
Basutoland, confusingly known as the 'High Commission Territories', or as 'British South Africa'. The trio,
containing between them about 1,200,000 Africans
and 10,000 Whites, are full of contradictions and para-
doxes. Though they are still under the direct 'protection' of the British Crown, their economic situation has
become interwoven with that of the Union. They are
administered by a High Commissioner who lives in
Pretoria and who combines his post with that of
Ambassador to South Africa—an anomalous dual role.
The Government headquarters of Bechuanaland are
actually in South Africa—in the small town of Mafe-
king, just across the border: those of Basutoland,
which is completely encircled by the Union, are only
just within the protectorate, in the border town of
Maseru: while Swaziland, the richest of the three, has
nearly half of its land owned by South Africans.

The existence of these British pockets in South
Africa dates from the time of union, when the British
Government felt unable to include them in the new
state, without the agreement or 'consultation' of the
inhabitants. All three territories had sought the

protection of Queen Victoria in the late nineteenth century—asking to be, in the picturesque words of the
Basuto King Mosesh, 'the fleas in the Queen's Blan-
ket'. Since the Union did not allow the franchise to
Africans except in the Cape Province, Britain insisted
on maintaining her trusteeship, but allowed, in the
controversial Section 151 of the Act of Union, for the
possibility of their transfer at a later date.

The clause was included in the expectation that
South Africa would become steadily more liberal in
its attitudes to Africans and their franchise—so that,
in the words of the then Colonial Secretary, Colonel
Seely, the transfer when it came 'may well be hardly
perceivable to the Natives themselves'. The Union
has, of course, developed in the opposite direction, so
that a transfer would easily be perceived. But the existence of the clause has been used by successive Union
Governments—and most vociferously since 1948—to
demand the incorporation of the protectorates. Their
reasons for wanting them are obvious : although they
are relatively poor, they are a reminder of freedom to
Africans across their borders, and their inclusion in
South Africa would increase the area of African lands,
or the projected 'Bantustans', to the more reasonable-
looking proportion, of sixty per cent.

The embarrassment for Britain, apart from the
strained relations with South Africa, lies in their
poverty and economic dependence on the Union. Africans from all of them have to migrate to South Africa
to earn a living, and wages of servants, clerks or
teachers are far lower in the protectorates. The choice
between money and tyranny, and poverty and freedom, is nowhere so marked as on the frontiers of the

protectorates: it is a sign of the impact of recent South African legislation that educated protectorate Africans have begun to return to their barren home-lands.

The three protectorates are alike only in their common predicament. The poorest of them, Bechuanaland, is a huge area five hundred miles square, consisting largely of the Kalahari Desert, but with a precious railway line on its eastern side, which Rhodes built to Rhodesia—carefully avoiding the (then Dutch republic of) Transvaal—which he called the 'Suez Canal to the north'. Bechuanaland became an acute problem to Britain in 1949, when the Paramount Chief designate, Seretse Khama, married an English girl. He was exiled to London by the British Labour Government, under pressure from South Africa, while his uncle, Tshekedi, was deposed from the Regency. Seven years later, under a Conservative Government, Seretse was allowed to return as a private citizen, having promised to renounce all claim to the chieftainship. A new tribal council was set up, with Seretse's cousin, Rasebolai, as Chairman, Seretse as Vice-Chairman and Tshekedi as Secretary—thus preparing a way to the development that the Bechuanas were demanding, a Legislative Council in place of the chieftaincy. At the same time, the prospect of considerable mineral development seemed to foreshadow an altogether new kind of society.

Swaziland, between Mozambique, Transvaal and Natal, is the richest territory of the three—with minerals, pasture-land, sugar and large forests. The protectorate is ruled by a bearded Swazi King, Sobhuza II, whose popularity with his people is helped by his ninety wives, who have connections with nearly every district. But the Swazis, through their 'Progressive Association', and even through the royal family, have given indications of wishing to develop to a more democratic system of government; and they have recently made more insistent demands for the land owned by Whites, which, they say, the Swazi King was tricked into giving away.

The most politically developed and educated of the three is Basutoland, the beautiful mountainous stronghold in the middle of South Africa. The 800,000 Basutos, who wear brightly coloured blankets and ride on sinewy ponies, are shrewd and clever people; they successfully defied troops from the Cape before their venerated King Mosesh sought Queen Victoria's protection. They combine strong nationalistic feelings with respect for their Chiefs and customs. The present Paramount Chieftainess, Mantsebo Seeiso—who acts as regent for her undergraduate nephew, Bereng—has allied herself with the Basuto National Congress, the local nationalist movement, in demanding representative government. It was the Basutoland Council, consisting largely of Chiefs, who in 1958 put forward proposals for a Legislative Council with limited self-government, which the British Government accepted. The news of the acceptance, which was greeted with bonfires on the hills of Basutoland, meant not only that Basutoland was moving towards an African state, but also that there could now be no question of incorporation—for the new council would have the right to decide on any future change in their country's status.

The new Basuto constitution gave great encouragement to the other two protectorates—particularly to

Bechuanaland—in their requests for self-government. South Africa, though she continued regularly to demand their incorporation, was surprisingly restrained in her reaction to Basuto self-government, and even suggested that it was in keeping with her own developments of *apartheid* and 'Bantustan'.

But the existence of genuinely self-governing states on the frontiers of the Union, even though they will remain financially dependent, must cause South Africa acute embarrassment, and will inevitably encourage nationalism within her borders. Their backwardness presents a difficult challenge to Britain and the Western critics of *apartheid*. Till recently, the protectorates have been the Cinderellas of British Africa, held back both by poverty and by fear of irritating South Africa. With more resources and international aid, they could influence the whole direction of Southern Africa.

*   *   *

A much less happy fate has attended the Western neighbour of South Africa, the arid rectangle of South West Africa, between Bechuanaland and the Atlantic. It was ruthlessly colonized by the Germans during the Scramble for Africa, who systematically deprived the inhabitants of their lands, and almost exterminated the most sophisticated of the tribes, the Hereros, reducing their population from 80,000 to 15,000. After the First World War—when the Hereros refused to fight with the Germans against South Africa—it became a League of Nations Mandate administered by South Africa, who increasingly claimed it as a logical part of their country. 'South West' (or 'West Africa' as South Africans often call it) still retains a very German

character and population, and its capital—Windhoek
—has beer-halls, German cafes and an *Allgemeine
Zeitung*. The territory is divided into two halves—the
'police zone' in the south, which contains nearly all the
50,000 Europeans, the towns and a valuable deposit of
diamonds at the mouth of the Orange River; and the
Native districts in the north, which are dry and
peopled by backward tribes dependent on the south
for money and work.

After the Second World War, the Mandate over the
half-million Africans was transferred to the United
Nations. But General Smuts, Prime Minister of South
Africa in 1946, refused to accept the right of the new
Trusteeship Council—which included a high proportion of non-European nations—to discuss the administration. South Africa feared, with reason, that debates
on South West Africa would extend to criticisms of the
'domestic policies' of the Union—as *apartheid* is
euphemistically called. The deadlock continued; after
1949 South Africa refused even to send reports to the
United Nations. The Herero tribe asked an Anglican
priest, Michael Scott, to represent their case, and for
the next ten years the wrangle continued. The International Court at The Hague decreed that the Union
could not modify South West Africa's international
status without consent of the United Nations; and the
United Nations appointed a special Committee to report on South West Africa, which, being prohibited
entry by South Africa, accepted what evidence they
could find from outside.

In November 1955 South Africa walked out altogether from the United Nations in protest against this
'interference': but three years later they returned, in

the hope that the new 'Good Offices Committee' which the UN had set up would pave the way to a reconciliation. The Good Offices Committee put forward a scheme for partition—giving the southern part to South Africa, and the northern part to UN Trusteeship—which was not surprisingly acceptable to South Africa. But the Trusteeship Council and the Hereros equally unsurprisingly rejected it, and the deadlock remained.

In the meantime the territory has become in its administration virtually part of South Africa, with even four nationalist MP's in the House of Assembly at Cape Town. Very little information has emerged about the conditions of Africans, and passports have been withheld from anyone likely to give news—including a young Herero offered a scholarship to Oxford. The present significance of the UN debates lies not so much in their hopes of being able to change South West Africa as in the opportunity for the rest of the world to criticize this frontier of *apartheid*. Although South Africa has maintained a stubborn posture, there have been hints that she has become more, not less, sensitive to world censure.

CHAPTER IX

THE FEDERAL FULCRUM

BETWEEN SOUTH AFRICA and the 'black north'
lies the trio of territories, shaped like a battered cottage
loaf, comprising the Central African Federation:
Southern and Northern Rhodesia, and Nyasaland.
Each territory has about two million Africans, and
they contain about three hundred thousand Europeans
in all, mostly concentrated in Southern Rhodesia.

The Federation, as it is more often called, embodies
nearly all the problems that assail the rest of Africa.
The conflicting interests of militant nationalism and
white and Asian minorities; missionaries and business-
men; settlers and colonial governments; tribal and
racial feuds—all press together in this central dilemma.
To the south is the perilous white fortress of South
Africa: on either side are the silent totalitarian colonies
of Portuguese East and West Africa: to the north is
black Tanganyika and the Congo. The Federation
mixes characteristics from each of them. It is one of
the very few entities in Africa without a port or a
coastline: it stands in landlocked isolation in the middle
of the African rumpus.

The creation of the Federation dates from 1953,
when, after long and bitter debates, the British House
of Commons finally voted in favour of the closer union
of the three territories. The gist of the objection was
the basic difference in status between the three com-
ponents, which had almost opposite origins. Southern

Rhodesia was annexed by the British South Africa Company, founded and urged forward by Cecil Rhodes, in the last years of the nineteenth century. There was no question of consulting the African's wishes in the appropriation of Rhodesia : Rhodes believed that the territory would contain a 'new Rand' of mineral wealth, that it would forestall German and Portuguese ambitions, and that it would act as a new British step from the Cape to Cairo. The mineral rights of Matabeleland, the southern portion of the territory, were obtained by the famous 'Rudd Concession' of 1888, in which the Matabele monarch Lobengula was tricked into selling the mineral rights—and as it turned out the whole territory—in exchange for £100 a month and a thousand Martini-Henry rifles with cartridges, together with a gunboat which never arrived. After two unsuccessful rebellions, the two million Africans of Southern Rhodesia have been among the most submissive and passive in the continent, and conquest shows in their faces. Since 1923 the territory has been governed by white settlers with their own small parliament, representing the white tenth (as it is now) of the population.

Northern Rhodesia was also annexed by the British South Africa Company, but not by force of arms : the Chiefs genuinely sought the protection of Queen Victoria, and the Company's rule passed not to the white settlers, but to the Colonial Office in London. Although there were unscrupulous agreements over the mineral rights in the copper area, where Belgians and British were both competing for Chiefs' signatures, it was not until the copper boom between the wars that the company's rights became valuable, and considerable white settlement began. Since the last war, when copper prices rocketed, Northern Rhodesia, like the Congo, has become far richer than the South, which is still largely agricultural. But white settlement is still restricted, and is concentrated along the 'line of rail' which leads from Southern Rhodesia to the Copperbelt, the 'new Rand' for which Rhodes was searching. Though the distinction between a colony and a protectorate often seems an academic one to Whites, it is one which Africans in the North never forget.

Even more disparate is the development of the smallest and poorest of the three, Nyasaland, which lies alongside the thin, long Lake Nyasa on the north-east of the Federation. For Nyasaland has been developed not so much by the British South Africa Company, which arrived there in 1889 and found nothing worth developing, as by the Church of Scotland, following in the wake of their greatest missionary, David Livingstone, who discovered Lake Nyasa in 1859. The Presbyterians founded their mission at Blantyre (named after Livingstone's birthplace) in 1875, before Rhodes had set foot in Rhodesia: and in spite of the poverty of the land, they formed a chain of mission schools which handed on to the enthusiastic Nyasas not only the Christian faith, but many Scots characteristics—toughness, independence, resilience and a passion for education. Although the average income is only £7 a year, education is almost as widespread as in the Rhodesias. The Nyasas are called by other Africans 'black Scotsmen', and have emigrated in large numbers, making their mark everywhere—in South Africa, Rhodesia and Kenya. Unlike the Rhodesians, Nyasaland has never really felt the full power and humiliation of commerce and the colour-bar: there are still only 7,000 Whites in the territory.

The discrepancy between the history of Nyasaland and Southern Rhodesia is not only the difference between the black and white poles of the Federation, but between the the principles of Rhodes and Livingstone. The two threads in Imperial history in Africa—commercial exploitation and missionary zeal—appear here in their most contrasted form.

It was these three strange bed-fellows that the Federation brought together. The motives behind the proposal—which (after being abandoned before the war) was put forward again by the Labour Government in 1950, then taken over by the Conservative Government in 1951—were sensible enough. The new state was to provide a great new economic unit which, with stability and a common market, would combine the white skills of Southern Rhodesia, the mineral wealth of Northern Rhodesia, and the manpower of Nyasaland. Africans, it was held, would benefit more than anyone from this new wealth. The objections of Africans in Northern Rhodesia and Nyasaland, that the terms of the protectorates were betrayed, were considered relatively unimportant, and based on ignorance.

The attractions of such a federation had become much greater since 1948, when Dr. Malan had come into power in South Africa with a policy less friendly to the British. The new Central African state could provide not only a defence against African nationalism from the west and east, but a 'bulwark' against the Afrikaner nationalism south of the Limpopo, the river which divides Rhodesia from the Union: it is a Rhodesian proverb that 'the Limpopo is a very narrow river'. The new union would have a more humane and less dangerous policy towards Africans. The 'Cape liberalism', which had withered in South Africa, would flower gradually in Central Africa, with Rhodes' policy of 'equal rights for all civilized men'. As an earnest of this difference, the word 'partnership' was written into the preamble of the Federal Constitution, as distinct from the *apartheid* of South Africa. To ensure the protection of Africans in Northern Rhodesia and Nyasaland, the Colonial Office was to retain the major control of the territories until at least 1960; and special safeguards were embedded in the constitution, including a special 'African Affairs Board', described by Oliver Lyttelton, the then Colonial Secretary, as an 'impregnable bastion', which had the right of appeal to the British Government against any discriminating Federal laws.

The Africans and their allies in Britain were not reassured. They were convinced that they were being betrayed into the hands of the white minority, and to them the scheme for Federation was not opposite, but parallel to the Union of South Africa forty years before. They remembered how the British Government had assured the critics of Union that the Boer republics would be 'liberalized' by the influence of the British Cape, and how the price of union had been the African vote.

There were other parallels between the Union in 1912 and Federation in 1953: for the Africans in Rhodesia were in much the same bewildered, half-tribal state as the Union Africans had been forty years earlier, with a tiny élite of leaders—including still only one black barrister in each of the three territories. But between the Whites of the Union and the Federation there was one essential difference : there was in Rhodesia no major racial cleavage, as between British and Afrikaner. Though there were around 40,000 Afrikaners in the Federation—notably in the Copper-belt —the English were in undisputed control. It comes as a relief to leave the bitter British-Dutch feuds of the Union for the more placid white society of Rhodesia : but this common Englishness provided what Africans had most dreaded in the Union—a united white front, which could easily be united against them.

The economic advantages of Federation soon showed themselves. As a visible sign of the new prosperity, the sleepy country town of Salisbury, the capital both of the Federation and of Southern Rhodesia, quickly transformed itself into a booming concrete city, growing faster than any other city in Africa. The price of copper—which provided forty per cent of the country's exports—stayed high enough, and investors who had been frightened away from the Union poured money into Central Africa. While Johannesburg's sky-line remained virtually the same—a sad monument to Afrikaner *apartheid*—skyscrapers pushed up between the old gingerbread shops of Salisbury. With abundant docile labour, a temperate climate, no death duties, and increasing sophistication, the Federal capital became a sunlit British playground, with the exciting challenge of a frontier, growth and untouched land.

In the peaceful streets of Salisbury, it is easy to forget about the colour problem : there is little of the sense of tension which makes Johannesburg an obviously unhappy place. Segregation in Salisbury is in

some ways more thorough than in South Africa, but
it is more discreet. Painful removals as in Sophiatown
have not been necessary, for Salisbury was planned
with the crowded black townships well away from the
white centre.

In social arrangements, too, there seemed to be signs
that 'partnership' would become a reality: the first
Federal parliament had six African MP's—later increased to twelve—sitting alongside the white members, and early in 1959 a junior black minister was
appointed to the Government. A small number of well-
educated Africans voted on the common roll with
Europeans, and under the new constitutional amendments of 1957—amendments of careful complexity—a
'special roll' was introduced to allow larger numbers of
Africans to have a limited vote. In Southern Rhodesia
new legislation allowed Africans to enter certain hotels,
enabled the one black barrister to practise in a white
area, and African students to live in the new multi-
racial university in Salisbury. Some of the 'pinpricks'—
as Whites optimistically call the iron that enters into
the African soul—were removed: barriers in shops and
offices were gradually taken down, a multi-racial club
and restaurant appeared, African policemen directed
white traffic, and the 'Europeans Only' signs on the
park seats in Salisbury faded. Educated Africans were
theoretically allowed to be served on railway dining-
cars: liberal Europeans in Salisbury played tennis with
Africans, swam with them, or invited them to dinner, in
a way that had been unthinkable ten years before. With
some reason the Whites claimed that the door to black
advancement was ajar, and not slammed as in South
Africa.

But the steel framework of white legislation, which governed the Africans' daily lives, remained largely unchanged. In Southern Rhodesia, 50 per cent of the land remained owned by the white tenth of the population, and no African could own land in urban areas. The new systems of franchise allowed the educated Africans the act of voting, without threatening the white minority. Most infuriating to the Africans, the black MP's in the Federal Parliament were elected by a predominantly *white* electorate. The creaming off of the black bourgeoisie, which the South Africans had neglected, has been partially accomplished in the Federation, producing 'white Africans' who were in some respects similar to the French *évolués* but who, being compelled to reject their people's following, were regarded by Africans as 'Quislings'.

While 'partnership' and 'multi-racialism' continued to be proclaimed, the apparently inexorable corruption of power worked on the white minority; the white electors, as in South Africa, voted for the extension of their white privileges, and bad politics drove out good. The 'impregnable bastion' of the African Affairs Board appealed twice to London against 'discriminatory' laws —the Constitution Amendment Act and the Electoral Bill of 1958. The appeals were rejected, one of the three members of the Board resigned, and the Federal Prime Minister attacked their 'interference', on the grounds that the changes had already been agreed with the British Government.

In Southern Rhodesia the 'liberal' Prime Minister, Garfield Todd, suffering under the political disadvantage of a missionary past, was eventually ousted by his colleagues, and in the election which followed in 1958 his policies were decisively rejected in favour of the firmer government of Sir Edgar Whitehead. In the Federal Parliament the eccentric founder of Federation, Lord Malvern, was succeeded as Prime Minister by a tough ex-trade unionist, Sir Roy Welensky, who made full use of the 'black bogy' in his electioneering, quickly arousing the fears of Africans. "Even in a hundred or two hundred years' time", he said, "the African shall never hope to dominate the Federation."

A huge, rugged man with a square jaw and a relaxed manner, Welensky easily attracted the confidence of white voters. The son of a Lithuanian Jew and his Afrikaner wife who had trekked up from South Africa, he was brought up in the slums of Salisbury, where by the age of eighteen he was heavyweight boxing champion of the Rhodesias. Later he emigrated to the railway town of Broken Hill in Northern Rhodesia, where he became an engine-driver and later head of the white railwaymen's trade union. His personality represents the dichotomy which runs through Rhodesian politics : he is on the one hand the ideal labour leader, with qualities reminiscent of Ernest Bevin ; but his experience in trades unions and railways has given him a sure instinct of the political importance of the colour bar. His shrewd political sense has now given him an almost unchallenged position in the Federal Parliament. He successfully took the wind out of the sails of his right-wing opposition, the Dominion Party—who urged a looser 'alliance' with Nyasaland and parts of Northern Rhodesia, while advocating sterner restrictions on the remaining Africans.

But while Federation was providing a united and prosperous white front, it was also—as Union had done in South Africa—providing a far stronger African front. The flaw in the whole Federal idea had been the disregard of African wishes : in so far that Africans had been consulted, they had rejected it. Most Europeans believed that Africans would soon become persuaded of the economic benefits of the new State, and that, like Africans in the Union, they would come to be proud of it. But Africans in the Federation were living in a far stormier political climate than pervaded the old days of South Africa. They had become powerfully aware of the ferment in the rest of Africa, and their own backwardness in the race for self-government.

The bastion of the new nationalism was Nyasaland, whose people had emigrated all over the Federation, setting the pace for African organization elsewhere. Nyasas faced few of the distractions from politics that affected Africans further south : though they certainly gained some economic benefits from Federal subsidies, these seemed unimportant compared to the threat of control from Salisbury. The Nyasaland African National Congress, first founded in 1950 with the slogan 'Kwaca' (awake), received a vast new following when Federation was put forward. Though splits occurred, the differences occurred only over the best means to fight Federation. In the words of the Devlin Commission, which later reported on the causes of the disturbances, there was 'a deep and bitter division of opinion separating the Government from the people'.

A surge of new militancy came with the return of an honoured Nyasa from England, Dr. Hastings Banda, in July 1958, when he was immediately elected President of Congress. Dr. Banda, a small brisk demagogue of fifty-three, typified the toughness of his

THE FEDERAL FULCRUM 171

people. At the age of thirteen he had walked a thousand miles to the gold mines of Johannesburg, where he earned enough money to reach America, and later to finish his medical degree at Edinburgh. He built up a prosperous white medical practice in Kilburn, and campaigned from London with other African leaders, including Kenyatta and Nkrumah, for the liberation of Africa. His surgery became the London headquarters of the Nyasa campaign against Federation: after a three years' stay in Ghana, he made his triumphant return to the country which he had left forty years before, to find a crowd of eight thousand waiting at the airport. His exile, and the fact that he had forgotten Nyasa languages, was a political advantage: he had all the status of the Western-educated man, together with a sharp, mercurial oratory which could switch instantly from mimicry to passion. He frequently condemned violence and boasted of his European friends, but his policy was uncompromising: "I am the extremest of extremists", he said: "to hell with Federation."

The anger of the Nyasas reverberated through the other two territories, over which were scattered branches of the Nyasaland Congress. In Northern Rhodesia African politics were more divided, and disabled by the rivalry between the African trades union leader, Laurence Katilungu, and the Congress President, the veteran easy-going Harry Nkumbula. But in October 1958 a section of the Northern Rhodesian African National Congress split off from its leader to form a more uncompromising body—the Zambia African Congress. The Zambia leader, Kenneth Kaunda, was an ascetic and dedicated ex-schoolteacher influenced, like some of his colleagues, by the example of India, and opposite in every way from the genial and worldly Nkumbula. As its first point of difference with the 'rump' of Congress, Zambia resolved to enforce a boycott of the 1959 Northern Rhodesian elections for which Nkumbula was standing.

Meanwhile politics in Southern Rhodesia were more placid: the Congress which had been founded in 1940 had lain dormant for years. But with the passing of new restrictive acts and the growing urbanization after Federation, political feeling grew, and in September 1957—on the anniversary of 'Occupation Day'—the dormant Congress was revived. Most of its impetus came from the 'Youth League', led by a volatile young bookkeeper, George Nyandoro, who represented the new urban intelligentsia.

It was clear that the four Congresses of the Federation were bound to come into conflict with the Federal Government.

The inevitable clash came in February 1959; a group of fifteen Africans in the Northern Province of Nyasaland were arrested for holding an illegal meeting, and an angry crowd stormed the jail and forced the release of the prisoners. Rioting immediately broke out in several parts of Northern Nyasaland: Africans put up road blocks, placed rocks on airfields, and ejected the wife of a local mine recruiting officer. Federal troops were flown in from the Rhodesias, and in the subsequent 'clean-up' fifty Africans were killed and a thousand members of Congress, including Dr. Banda, were detained.

A few days after the first outbreaks in Nyasaland, five hundred members of Congress in Southern Rhodesia were arrested. A state of emergency was declared by the Prime Minister, Sir Edgar Whitehead, who alleged that the Congress was intimidating and terrorizing moderate African leaders—particularly MP's. A few weeks later legislation was introduced which made Congress illegal, and which enabled the Government to detain their opposition without trial for up to five years—a stronger measure than South Africa had ever introduced.

Meanwhile, the Governor of Northern Rhodesia ordered the arrest of thirty-eight leaders of the Zambia Congress, charging them with organizing a 'Murder Incorporated' to intimidate Africans from voting in the following week's elections. Thus, by the end of the month, only one of the four Congresses remained legal —the 'rump' of the Northern Rhodesian Congress, led by Harry Nkumbula.

The justification of these arrests was, to Whites, a plausible and even a liberal one : the Governments, like the French in Algeria, were not prepared to allow their plans for gradual partnership and economic advancement to be blocked by a small band of nationalist agitators.

But in the fluid state of Africa all round the frontiers of the Federation, there were growing doubts as to whether nationalism could be so easily contained. The liberals of the Federation, in the form of the new Central African Party founded in 1958 by Garfield Todd and Sir John Moffat, believed there was still a little time in which Europeans could, by massive concessions, regain the trust of Africans. But whether Nyasaland, after watching the incursions and shootings by Federal troops, could be held within the Federation, even when promised self-government, was more doubtful than ever: and if Nyasaland were to secede, Africans in Northern Rhodesia would insist on following.

The dilemma of Nyasaland became a major issue in British politics after the publication of the report of the four-man commission headed by Mr. Justice Devlin, which had been appointed to investigate the causes of the disturbances in March. The commissioners found, in the course of their 80,000 word report, that the opposition to Federation was deeply rooted and almost universal in Nyasaland: that the territory had become, since the emergency, a police state: that, although the Government were justified in declaring an emergency, there was nothing that 'can be called a plot': that Dr. Banda would never have approved a policy of murder: and that 'unnecessary and therefore illegal force' was used in making many of the arrests. After a bitter debate in the House of Commons, the British Government refused to accept those parts of the Devlin Report which did not endorse their policy, and Dr. Banda and his chief followers remained in jail. But the combination of the Report, the riots, and the new distrust of Sir Roy Welensky, produced a growing scepticism in Britain as to the merits of an independent Federation.

The disparate and distrustful trio of the Federation is a microcosm of most of the problems of Africa. They will also be Britain's last great problem in the continent, the hard core of her African Empire. In the liberalization of the Commonwealth, Britain has followed two paths—the earlier path to self-government of people of British stock, as typified by Canada or Australia, and the later path to self-government of coloured peoples, such as India. In Africa these two principles have come into tragic conflict. In South Africa, the British people were given autonomy with the Afrikaners fifty years ago: in Kenya, the autonomy will almost certainly be given to the native people. Only in Central Africa will Britain's responsibility linger, to hold some balance between White and Black.

10